971.533 R
390830277
Rees, Ron
Historic

HISTORIC
ST ANDREWS

IMAGES *of our Past*

HISTORIC
ST ANDREWS

RONALD REES

NIMBUS
PUBLISHING

CHARLOTTE COUNTY ARCHIVES

Copyright © Ronald Rees, 2001

All rights reserved. No part of this book may be reproduced, stored in a retrieval system or transmitted in any form or by any means without the prior written permission from the publisher, or, in the case of photocopying or other reprographic copying, permission from CANCOPY (Canadian Copyright Licensing Agency), 1 Yonge Street, Suite 1900, Toronto, Ontario M5E 1E5.

Nimbus Publishing Limited
PO Box 9166, Halifax, NS   B3K 5M8
(902) 455-4286

Design: Joan Sinclair
Printed and bound in Canada

Front cover:
On the corner of King and Montague streets in St Andrews stands Chestnut Hall, built c.1810 in the American Federal style for Christopher Hatch, a successful merchant and commander of the militia.

Title page:
LITHOGRAPH OF ST ANDREWS
after a sketch by Lieutenant Frederick Wells of the 1st Royals, c.1840
Instruction in drawing "ground" was part of every officer's training at the Woolwich Academy, London. When in the field, officers were required to study topography and be able to sketch defensive positions. Clearly, Lieutenant Wells was far more than a journeyman topographer. His accomplished sketch is the earliest comprehensive view of the town. The waterfront is crowded with wharves, warehouses, and shipyards and there are vessels in the harbour. On the approaches to the town, long, narrow farm lots run down to the river. In the distance, across the bay, are Deer Island and the coast of Maine.

Canadian Cataloguing in Publication Data
Rees, Ronald, 1935-
    Historic St. Andrews
    Images of Our Past
    Includes bibliographical references.
    ISBN 1-55109-357-X
1. St. Andrews (N.B.)-History. 2. St. Andrews (N.B.)-History-Pictorial works. I. Title. II. Series
FC2499.S35R43 2001   971.5'33   C2001-900346-3
F1044.5.S13R43 2001

We acknowledge the financial support of the Government of Canada through the Book Publishing Industry Development Program (BPIDP) and the Canada Council for our publishing activities.

Dedication

To Sheila Simpson

Acknowledgements

This book rests on the painstaking work of acquisition, description, and cataloguing conducted over thirty years by the curators, most of them volunteers, of the photo collection of the Charlotte County Archives in St Andrews. The current curators, Charlotte McAdam, Irene Scarratt, and Lila Haughn, not only guided me through the collection but did so with enthusiasm and unfailing good humour. Irene Scarratt was also kind enough to read the manuscript.

I am also a beneficiary of the remarkable powers of observation and recall of two of the town's senior residents, Harry Mallory and George Goodeill. All questions about the life of St Andrews in the first half of the last century lead directly to their doors. For information on the history of the businesses of Water Street, I am indebted to a source closer to home—my wife and helpmate Diana Rees.

Contents

Introduction ix

Chapter 1
    Houses and Residential Streets 1

Chapter 2
    Water Street 15

Chapter 3
    The Waterfront 35

Chapter 4
    Men in Uniform 51

Chapter 5
    Churches, Schools, and Public Buildings 65

Chapter 6
    Bands and Parades 79

Chapter 7
    Summer Hotels 95

Chapter 8
    Summer Houses 105

Notes 116

Introduction

The plaque that commemorates St Andrews' designation as a national historic district stands about two hundred feet from the point on the shore where the founders of the town are thought to have landed in October 1783. Legend has it that they arrived at low water and their goods and chattels, which they piled on the shore, had to be moved three times to avoid being swamped by the advancing tide. In this detail only—the phenomenal tidal range in the Bay of Fundy—the leaders and planners of the settlement had failed the new settlers. The latter were members of the Penobscot Association, a group of merchants, tradesmen, and professionals who had remained loyal to the Crown during the Revolutionary War (1775-1783). Originally from Falmouth (now Portland, Maine), Boston, and New York, the group had moved to Castine, then a British stronghold

ST CROIX, OR DOCHET'S ISLAND, 1889

Almost two centuries before the arrival of the Loyalists, Sieur de Monts and Samuel de Champlain sailed with a group of artisans, merchants, and seamen from northwestern France to La Cadie, the region of North America between the 40th and 46th parallels. Their aim was to colonize and govern, and to provide enough furs to satisfy the backers of the enterprise. In late June 1604, they settled on a small island about four miles above the mouth of the St Croix. During the harsh winter that followed, scurvy ravaged the company, killing thirty-four from the complement of seventy-nine. When a relief vessel arrived in the early summer of 1605, the chastened survivors abandoned the settlement in favour of a sheltered site at the mouth of the Annapolis River in Nova Scotia. Though a failure, the St Croix settlement was the first attempt by Europeans to establish a permanent, year-round settlement on the Atlantic coast north of the Spanish settlements in Florida.

protected by Fort George on the coast of what is present-day Maine. From Castine the merchants continued to trade with the British West Indies in the expectation that at the end of the war the Penobscot River would divide British and American territory. But at the Treaty of Paris, the American negotiators were in no mood to give up what is now eastern and northern Maine, nor were they willing to tolerate on American soil what the most unyielding of them characterized as "the viperine nest at Penobscot." When the news reached Castine that the St Croix River, not the Penobscot, was to be the international boundary, the Penobscot Loyalists had to prepare to move again.

Agents were appointed from among the Penobscot Loyalists to organize the evacuation and find an alternative location in British-controlled territory. As primarily a merchant group, their objective was to find a location from which they could carry on the lucrative British and West Indian trade. The best sites on the Nova Scotia peninsula had already been taken, so the scouts and agents focused their attention on the Bay of Fundy and what is now the New Brunswick shore. By August 1783 they had settled for a sloping peninsular site at the point where the St Croix enters the protected waters of Passamaquoddy Bay, a large inlet of the Bay of Fundy. Conditions at Castine, which lies on an isthmus at the point where the Penobscot River empties into the sheltered waters of Penobscot Bay, had been virtually duplicated.

To prepare for the arrival of the Loyalists, a townsite had to be surveyed and farm lots laid out along the river and the shores of the bay. The surveyors, led by Charles Morris Jr., son of the Surveyor-General of Nova Scotia, were instructed to lay out a town plan that was both "agreeable to the wishes" of the Loyalist agents and in line with the general instructions for the plotting of townsites issued by the Board of Trade and Plantations in London. The site itself was copy-book—a south-facing slope angling gently down to a river and a bay. In the survey, geometry prevailed. As in all colonial town planning, the objective was a plan simple enough to be carried out by two or three men equipped with a compass, a chain, and a level. Surveying began in mid-August and ended in late September. The resulting plan was a rectangle a mile long and half a mile deep, subdivided by a grid of streets either sixty or eighty feet wide. The only breaks in the grid were open squares for a marketplace and public buildings such as churches, schools, and a courthouse. In coastal towns the marketplace was to be at the halfway point of the street closest to the shore. Building lots, except for those running down to the shore, were standard in size: 80 x 160 feet. Shore lots were much narrower to give as many merchants as possible access to the water. As was customary in colonial towns, land on the edges of the plat was set aside for common pasturage and military use.

QUEEN CHARLOTTE AND GEORGE III

As the reigning monarchs at the time of the Loyalist exodus, George III and Queen Charlotte were bound to cast a long shadow in places where the Loyalists settled. The province itself is named after the House of Brunswick, and Charlotte County after the Queen. Reproductions of the portraits of the royal children that hang in the long gallery of Windsor Castle can be found in the Charlotte County Courthouse in St Andrews. Thirteen of the streets in St Andrews are named after the royal children.

Except for Water Street, the street closest to the shore, the remaining street names had either royal or colonial associations. King—the show street—Queen, Princess Royal, and the Prince of Wales need no explanation, but thirteen of the remainder are named after the children of George III, from Augustus and Ernest to Mary and Patrick. Two other streets were named Parr and Carleton; Colonel John Parr was the governor of Nova Scotia, and Sir Guy Carleton was the commander in chief of the king's forces in North America. St Andrews was a symbol of the British monarchy as well as a settlement for the king's loyal subjects.

The first contingent of settlers arrived on October 3, 1783, in two large transports and several smaller vessels. In all, roughly a thousand would make the journey from Castine to St Andrews, about 650 civilians of the Penobscot Association and 200-300 disbanded soldiers, fewer than half of whom had wives. Settlers bound for the new town drew lots before embarkation. One of them, Nathaniel Palmer, mentions being present at "a General Drawing of Town Lotts by the settlers for the New Town of St Andrews." The Penobscot agents, organizers of the last major Loyalist settlement in the Maritimes, had before them the negative examples of Shelburne and Saint John where, in each case, the evacuees arrived either during the survey or before it had even begun. The result was an unseemly and chaotic scrambling for lots. On arrival at St Andrews, by contrast, the evacuees were met by members of a settlement committee who directed them to their lots, each of which was designated by division, lot number, and letter. For late arrivals and industrious squatters, magistrates had the power to allocate lots not yet taken up and, when more land was needed, they applied to Halifax for a twenty rod extension along the entire back of the town. To prevent speculation in lots, each grantee had to build within a year a building at least sixteen feet square and "exactly six feet from the street."

For the forty years after the founding, the town prospered. As the shiretown, or county seat, of Charlotte County, St Andrews had an important administrative role, but first and foremost it was a merchant settlement. There was little interest in farming as food could always be imported if necessary. Adult males and heads of households were entitled to a farm or "garden" lot of one hundred acres, though many of these lots were not taken up and if they were, they were often used only as sources of lumber. In February 1785, Matthew Lymburner, a disgruntled farmer, despaired of a town that he found had "a sufficient accommodation for Artizans" but not for farming folk. The traders and merchants had eyes only for the lucrative West Indian trade and their chief objective was to take control of the market by eliminating American competition. In order to achieve this monopoly, Britain had to be persuaded to enforce navigation laws which stipulated that, barring emergencies, goods destined for British or imperial markets had to be carried in British vessels. But first, British officials needed to be convinced that British North America could supply West Indian planters with all the fish, lumber, and naval stores they needed.

Confident assertions were the order of the day. Robert Pagan, a prominent St Andrews merchant, saw no need to involve the rest of British North America in the West Indian trade. Except for oak staves, which were used to make barrels, Pagan declared that "the Grand Bay of Passsamaquoddy alone [could] supply the whole British West India Islands with Boards, Planks, Scantling, Ranging Timber, Shingles [and] Clapboards." Supplies of masts, spars, and square timber for the British market would, as he saw it, be limited only by "the want of inhabitants and saw mills." Pagan seemed as good as his word. By the end of May 1785, the Penobscot Loyalists had sent off their first cargoes of lumber and fish, and in return came rum, molasses, sugar, and salt. Lumber was also shipped to Britain in quantities that increased dramatically when Napoleon closed the Baltic Sea to British shipping and cut off supplies of Swedish lumber. Duties against colonial lumber fell as lumber prices in Britain soared, and were further reduced early in the nineteenth century when Thomas Jefferson cut off United States lumber supplies to the British market.

The cheapest way of getting lumber to overseas markets was to build ships to carry it and to sell both ships and cargo on arrival. So began the shipbuilding industry in St Andrews and St Stephen. On outgoing tides it is said that the St Croix was often white with sail as merchantmen and fishing vessels made for Britain, the West Indies, and fishing banks offshore. Waterfronts were lined with wharves, ships, warehouses, and chandleries, and the men who manned or frequented them were often more familiar with Liverpool and Havana than with neighbouring towns in Maine and New Brunswick.

Despite Robert Pagan's boast, neither Passamaquoddy nor the Maritimes as a whole could fill British needs for lumber, naval stores, and foodstuffs. Britain and the West Indies still needed American raw materials and the United States was equally dependent upon British manufacturers. To circumvent the navigation laws, vessels from St Andrews and other Maritime ports became carriers of American goods, and during periods of hostility between Britain and the United States, shipowners in St Andrews and around the bay served as go-betweens by transferring goods between British and American vesssels. The exchange took place "along the lines," the indeterminate border zone between British and American waters. Goods, too, were stored in St Andrews and on islands in the bay, and, under cover of darkness or fog, ferried to Robbinston, Lubec, or Eastport. Detection was difficult if not impossible in the island-studded bay, and for the first half of the nineteenth century smuggling was a way of life.

While British markets remained protected and American vessels continued to be denied access to British ports, St Andrews prospered. It was, however, a fragile prosperity as it depended entirely on British favour or magnanimity. Patrick Campbell, an astute Scottish observer, had seen the danger of protectionism as early as 1794. He allowed that St Andrews was "prettily situated" and had a "smart trade" in shipbuilding, lumber, and fish, but he noted direly that this standing could be maintained only as long as Americans were kept out of British markets. If Britain were to repeal its navigation laws and embrace free trade, then, Campbell predicted, St Andrews could not subsist. The first blow fell in the 1830s when Britain opened West Indian markets to American shipping. Within the three years between 1830 and 1834, St Andrews's exports to the West Indies (more than half its annual exports) fell by two-thirds. The British lumber market remained protected until 1842, but by this date lumbering on the St Croix had moved well upstream. There were still marketable trees around St Andrews but most were in tracts held by the Royal Navy. The loss of the lumber trade inevitably affected shipbuilding. Although slow at first, the decline became headlong when steam and iron began to replace wood and sail. Boats were still built for the coastal trade and the fishery, but the demand could not sustain a major industry.

With the loss of the Atlantic trade, St Andrews—which had once been an important link in the commerce of the Atlantic—found itself in a remote corner of a continent that was increasingly preoccupied with the development of its own interior. As early as 1836 the historian Peter Fisher noted that the town's trade "appear[ed] to be dwindling away without any satisfactory prospect of revival." To stop the rot, a group of businessmen struck on the vaulting idea of making St Andrews the winter port of Canada by building a railway to Quebec, thus circumventing the frozen St Lawrence River. Funds were raised and a route surveyed, but work on the project halted abruptly when Americans discovered that the builders intended to run the line through disputed territory between Maine and New Brunswick. The Webster/Ashburton Treaty of 1842 settled the dispute, but not before Saint John and Halifax had decided that they, too, would make excellent Atlantic termini. Construction of the St Andrews/Quebec line began in 1847 but the projected line was never completed.

For St Andrews, the railway to the interior, which promised to marry the new continental economy to the old Atlantic one, was the last effort at a vital, workaday existence. In the 1850s, a correspondent to a Fredericton newspaper described St Andrews as the most somnolent place he had ever set foot in, the main street deathly quiet and the harbour empty except for a ship unloading rails and an old dismasted schooner lying at one of the wharves. In 1860, a visitor returning after a twelve-year interval found the town to be "dull, dilapidated, and in need of paint." Idle men, looking like "shipwrecked sailors on a deserted isle," rambled dejectedly about the streets and wharves, and a shore that was once alive with sail became a catchpit for unwanted schooners and barges. As the town's economy collapsed, people drifted away. By 1880 the population had fallen to its current level, fewer than two thousand, a figure perhaps half that at the beginning of the nineteenth century.

Yet in spite of the collapse of its economy, St Andrews escaped obliteration. The founders had chosen better than they realized. A remote peninsular location might have proved painfully vulnerable to the collapse of the Atlantic trade, but a town—as even the very practical Patrick Campbell felt bound to remark—so "prettily situated" had distinct advantages for one of the growth industries of the nineteenth and twentieth centuries: tourism. When the prominent Loyalist Edward Winslow, suffering from an attack of gout, visited in 1810, he was effusive, declaring the town and the settting to be "by far the most interesting and delightful part of the province of New Brunswick." In 1871 Sir Leonard Tilley, the leader of New Brunswick's reluctant movement toward joining the Confederation, became a summer resident. A Saint John editor accused him of "burrowing" in some town along the border but within a year Sir Charles Tupper, who for a season was the prime minister of Canada, had followed Sir Leonard's example.

By 1881 there were two summer hotels, and a hotel company floated by ratepayers who voted to increase their assessment by $10,000. Visitors were attracted both by the scenery and by air cooled by the huge tidal changes in the bay. Water temperatures never rise above a chilling 50F. Summers in St Andrews are not only cool but, if measured by relative humidity, dry and virtually mosquito-free. For the wealthy of Boston, New York, Philadelphia, and Montreal, the Gulf of Maine and the Bay of Fundy were irresistible. They offered escape not just from heat and humidity but also from disease. Until Pasteur demonstrated in the 1860s that diseases were transmitted by micro-organisms, there was no certain knowledge of the causes of infection, and no adequate treatment for infectious disease. The most widespread belief, which persisted until the end of the century, was that the agents of disease were airborne poisons or "miasmas" generated spontaneously either in chambers beneath the earth's surface or in fetid places above. On the surface, miasma-producing conditions were thought to be warm air, moisture, and decaying animal and vegetable matter, and so hot and humid places were considered unhealthy, and cool, dry places healthy.

Seasonal migrations to escape tropical heat, humidity, and diseases such as malaria and yellow fever began in the eighteenth century, but not until the development of railways in the mid-nineteenth century would they assume the proportions of an exodus. Along the eastern seaboard, summer resorts for the urban rich crept steadily up the coast, reaching Mount Desert Island and Bar Harbor by the 1870s, and Campobello and the Bay of Fundy by 1881. With rail connections to Boston after 1871, and Montreal after 1889, St Andrews was an obvious choice for development as a fashionable resort. The investors were chiefly Bostonians and Montrealers, with railway and steamship connections, who floated a land company in 1888, and a year later built a large summer hotel—the Algonquin—on a plateau overlooking the town.

In 1889 the Canadian Pacific Railway (CPR) acquired both the New

Brunswick and Quebec railway, which connected St Andrews with central Canada, and the European and North American Railway, which linked Boston and Bangor with Saint John. The lines crossed at the remote lumber town of McAdam where, to accommodate passengers switching to or from the St Andrews branch line, CPR built a massive station hotel in its turreted, chateau style. Within a few years CPR acquired the Algonquin and, with it, the holdings of the St Andrews Land Company. Then, as a matter of course, it took over the promotion of the town. With confidence in conventional medicine still low, two of St Andrews's attributes were stressed: the healthfulness of the climate and the ample opportunities for outdoor recreation. Sufferers from nervous conditions, chest complaints, and hay fever (the latter seen then as a malady of well-to-do Anglo Saxons) could vacation here with impunity.

Until the 1930s and 1940s, St Andrews was an exclusive resort for rich, or at least affluent, Anglo-Saxon Americans and Canadians. Insulated by wealth and social status, they savoured for a few months each summer the class privileges that were theirs in the cities. Visitors came for a month or a season, and if they owned summer houses, they were accompanied by an entourage of maids, cooks, chauffeurs, and even butlers. To prepare for their arrival, dusty streets were watered down and, in the case of visiting dignitaries, band instruments tuned and readied. All this changed, however, with the invention of an affordable automobile and the growing wealth and confidence of the middle classes. Today, the owners of summer houses still come for the season, but guests at the hotels and motels stay for a day or a week and are much more likely to arrive by family car and chartered bus than by chauffered limousine.

Chapter 1

Houses and Residential Streets

CHESTNUT HALL

The intersection of King and Montague streets, according to at least one historian of architecture, is the most distinguished street corner in Canada. On three of the corners are fine Georgian or Neoclassical houses, and on the fourth a handsome Anglican church. The style of Chestnut Hall is American Federal, yet another elaboration of Georgian, with a hipped roof, balanced façade, and chimneys symmetrically arranged on each of the four corners. Each of the principal rooms has a marble fireplace and is decorated with elaborate plasterwork. Chestnut Hall was built c.1810 for Christopher Hatch, a successful merchant and commander of the militia, who gave lavish parties crowned by sumptuous meals provided by Violet, his black cook. Many of the Loyalists arrived with black slaves and indentured servants. In 1938/39 Chestnut Hall was bought by Henry Phipps Ross and Sarah Juliette Phipps Ross and given to the town as a museum for the conservation and display of their private collection of furniture and decorative art.

PANORAMIC VIEW, 1896

Like most of the Loyalist towns, St Andrews grew quickly. The refugees complained of the slow arrival of the tools, equipment, and lumber promised by the British, but within six months of the town's founding, Robert Pagan was able to write that there were "about Ninety houses up, and great preparations making in every quarter of the town for more." By 1788, more than 250 houses had been built, accommodating well over a thousand people. Although some settlers were forced to spend the first few winters in bark huts and other crude shelters, the Loyalists tended to build well-made structures from the outset so that their towns never had the makeshift look of frontier towns elsewhere. During the forty years which preceded this photograph, there had been little new building, and existing buildings, although in need of paint, were intact. In 1890 a correspondent for the *Boston Home Journal* described the town as "the ruins of a once lively fishing port now passed into a dream." Most of the buildings exhibit characteristic Georgian features: compactness, good proportions, and simple outlines.

JEREMIAH POTE'S HOUSE

BOTTOM RIGHT

A distinguished French geographer once remarked that emigrants carry their shells with them. By this he meant that in the new land they almost invariably reproduce the kind of houses they had known at home. Many of the Penobscot emigrants went a step further. Warned of shortages of lumber and other building materials in Shelburne and Saint John, many of them dismantled their Castine houses, numbered the framing timbers, and loaded the timbers, boards, doors, and windows onto scows that were towed behind the transports. On arrival the pieces were taken to the owner's assigned house lot and reassembled. In general, salt-box houses, which probably grew out of the primitive lean-to and therefore suggest folk or peasant origins, had no great appeal for the Loyalists. Originally from Falmouth (Portland, Maine), Jeremiah Pote was a prominent merchant, and one of the agents chosen by the Penobscot Association to find a new location for the Castine Loyalists and plan a method of settlement.

THE LOYALIST HOUSE

The Loyalist house, so called because it is one of the few survivors among the houses brought from Castine, could well be the oldest house in St Andrews. According to one account, the Montague Street house was built in Castine in 1770, and dismantled and shipped to St Andrews in 1783. Another has it that the house was built afresh from frames and timber brought from Falmouth. For some years the merchant Robert Pagan used the building as a store, but for most of its life it has been a dwelling. Repairs after two separate fires revealed walls that were made of split boards—not laths—covered with plaster bonded with cow hair. The small vestibule in the front was a traditional feature.

JEREMIAH POTE'S HOUSE

THE RIGBY HOUSE

A one-and-a-half-storey house with a central doorway and one or two windows evenly spaced on each side was the standard folk house of the region. Low walls and tight eaves made for ease and efficiency of heating while the large roof gave the house a snug, sheltering look. The second storey nestled beneath the roof. The house's nearest European relations were seventeenth-century cottages in parts of England and Scotland. The house in this photograph, at the junction of Edward and Prince of Wales Streets, has an ell and beyond the ell a barn and a paddock. In the distance is the roof of the old Algonquin Hotel. The Algonquin opened in 1889.

ROBERT GARNETT'S HOUSE

TOP RIGHT

Elongated one-and-a-half-storey houses, built in sections, were a popular Loyalist type. One obvious advantage of this style is that they were easy to extend. When a brother-in-law of the late nineteenth-century owners (the McConvey family) drowned at sea in 1881, his widow and four young children were housed in an addition built for them. In this photograph, which was taken in the early 1940s, the building is being demolished to provide an unobstructed view of the harbour for owners who bought the lot and eventually built a new house. As in the case of the Loyalist house, the components for the Garnett house came from Castine.

DUNN-MCQUOID HOUSE

BOTTOM RIGHT

John Dunn's classically proportioned (Georgian) house might have been the first two-storey dwelling built in St Andrews. When he fled from New York, Dunn, like many of the Castine refugees, took the precaution of bringing building materials with him. Although more elaborate than the storey-and-a-half folk houses, Dunn's Water Street house is plain, even austere. Dunn became Sheriff of Charlotte County and for many years he was Collector of Customs, ostensibly a rewarding position in a community where smuggling was a way of life. Restored and refurbished in the 1970s by the St Andrews Civic Trust and the New Brunswick Housing Corporation, the building is now apartments for senior citizens.

ROBERT GARNETT'S HOUSE

DUNN-MCQUOID HOUSE

5   Houses and Residential Streets

PAGAN-O'NEILL HOUSE

Robert Pagan was a Scotsman from Glasgow and one of four brothers who came to North America. In Falmouth (Portland), he joined a firm that sold lumber and ships to Great Britain and the West Indies but, as a vociferous supporter of the Crown, he was forced to seek shelter in Fort George. Of all the Penobscot Loyalists he was the most determined to secure the colonial preference for British North American goods. In St Andrews he became a prominent merchant, a magistrate, a judge, a member of the Legislative Assembly, and a colonel in the militia. His wife, Miriam, was the daughter of Jeremiah Pote. In the 1830s the Queen Street house was bought by Henry O'Neill, a butcher from Ireland who established a thriving and long-lived grocery and general store on the site now occupied by the town's only supermarket. Like most of the Castine houses, the Pagan-O'Neill house has seen many structural changes. Only what is now the ell, which fronts on Frederick Street, and the roof boards, which run vertically rather than horizontally, are thought to have been part of the original structure.

THE SHERIFF ANDREWS/HIBBARD HOUSE

BOTH PHOTOS AT RIGHT

Either for reasons of economy or from the need to build quickly, most of the early houses were plain, well-proportioned buildings designed to see the refugees through the difficult initial period of settlement. For their replacement houses, the merchants and professional men opted for large town houses in the neoclassical style, an elaboration of simple or basic Georgian. Doorways had sidelights as well as fanlights; the fanlights tended to be more elaborate, and windows were shuttered. In neoclassical as in Georgian houses, proportion and symmetry were all-important. Shapes, as in the smaller folk houses, were rectangular and façades balanced. Interiors were just as regular as exteriors, each floor having a pair of rooms of roughly equal size on each side of a usually spacious central hallway and staircase. Exteriors were usually of clapboard, with wide corner boards and solid, generous eaves. Several owners, however, opted for the more impressive, and—especially if home made—more expensive, brick. Both finished and rough bricks came from Britain in vessels returning in ballast (i.e. without a full cargo) but the rough bricks were used only as a filler between the studs. Fine bricks were also made in town either with clay dug from the foundations or, more probably, with clay from a clay pit on the shore west of the town.

The house (bottom photo) was built on King Street c.1820, at the height of the town's prosperity, by Elisha Andrews, Sheriff of Charlotte County and son of the Reverend Samuel Andrews, the town's first Anglican rector. Servants lived upstairs in attic rooms connected to the living and dining rooms, and to the basement kitchen by a back staircase.

The photograph at right shows the commanding central doorway with its elegant arched fanlight. The figures are George Franklin Hibbard and Julia Etta Hibbard, who bought the house in 1900. George Hibbard was a merchant, a member of the legislature, and registrar of deeds and wills for the county. The Hibbard family owned the house until 1985 when it was bought by A. Murray Vaughan of St Andrews and given to the province. Refurbished in the style of the early nineteenth century, the house is now a museum.

GEORGE FRANKLIN HIBBARD AND JULIA ETTA HIBBARD, 1900.

Houses and Residential Streets

HARRIS HATCH HOUSE

Around 1840, Harris Hatch, the son of Christopher Hatch, built this impressive townhouse on Queen Street. Even for a time when property and appointment-seeking were the main preoccupations, Harris Hatch cut a broad swath. He was by turns lawyer, businessman, registrar of deeds, president of the Charlotte County Bank and of the St Andrews-Quebec Railway Company, magistrate, member of the Legislative Assembly, and colonel in the militia. The porch, which conceals a fine central doorway with sidelights and an arched fanlight, was a Victorian addition. The windows of the porch and the exterior glass door have since been removed but the portico remains.

GREENOCK HOUSE
TOP RIGHT

Structurally, Greenock house is said to have much in common with Chestnut Hall but differs from it in having an offset doorway. The Edward Street house has always been associated with nearby Greenock Church as the lot it occupies was to have been the site for a manse built by the church's mercurial benefactor, the merchant Christopher Scott. Work on the manse started shortly after the completion of the church in 1824, but a slump in trade, and the decision by the minister for whom it was intended to house himself elsewhere, halted construction. Subsequently the property was transferred to William Scott, whom Christopher Scott described as "my reputed illegitimate son," then sold to George D. Street. Q.C. Street completed the building c.1830.

THE ANCHORAGE c.1889
BOTTOM RIGHT

Built on Parr Street in 1825 as a rectory for the first Roman Catholic priest, the house now known as The Anchorage remained in church hands until 1880. Under the church's ownership one of the downstairs ceilings, in a room probably used as a private chapel, was painted in a colourful Italianate style. In 1897, ownership passed to Thomasina Andrews and her husband Captain Frederick Andrews, both mariners. Thomasina Andrews, who went to sea frequently with her husband, is thought to have been one of the first women to receive navigational papers. Appropriately for seafarers, they named the house The Anchorage.

GREENOCK HOUSE

THE ANCHORAGE

Houses and Residential Streets

LOWER KING STREET

For greater regularity, houses in St Andrews, as in the Loyalist towns generally, were required to be "even in line" with the street and, in the case of St Andrews, "exactly six feet" from it. Long setbacks were a requirement of nineteenth-century planning. Away from the centre, the houses stood alone on large lots, but close to Water Street and the shore, where space was at a premium, houses tended to stand shoulder to shoulder on subdivided lots. An occasional house might show its gable end, or even its back, to the street, with the main entrance opening onto a lawn or an enclosed garden, but in general the houses looked outward. In this photograph of lower King Street, the building in the right foreground is the Hibbard/Sheriff Andrews house; in the right backround is the Anglican Church.

UPPER KING STREET SCENES

PHOTOS AT RIGHT

When all movement of goods and people was by water, houses and commercial buildings crowded onto the shore. A few blocks from the shore conditions were semi-rural, the streets unimproved, and the houses scattered; by the late nineteenth century, houses were hidden by a screen of chestnuts and elms. The three cyclists in the top photo, right, perform their balancing act just two blocks north of Water Street. To the left is a rail fence. Bert Armstrong, the central figure on the "pennyfarthing," became a dentist and went to the Klondike (c.1898) with Will Carson and Tom Black, two other St Andrews men.

Farther up the street conditions were even more rural. The fenced area to the left is the Loyalist burying ground, located on land given to the town for the purpose by Jeremiah Pote.

UPPER KING STREET SCENES

Houses and Residential Streets

SOPHIA STREET LOOKING NORTH

Sophia Street is only four blocks east of King and Water, the town centre, yet building density is already low. The building to the right is a barn, or livery stable, the nineteenth century's equivalent of the present-day garage. The house in the left foreground is one of several of this type built between 1850 and 1870. Georgian compactness and regularity have been retained but the steep roof and the sharply-angled gable are concessions to Perpendicular or Gothic styles.

MILTON HALL

TOP RIGHT

Frustrated by what they regarded as the Georgian or classical straitjacket, architects in the middle of the nineteenth century began to experiment with freer forms that allowed greater latitude in the arrangement of rooms and the design of exteriors. Accents shifted to the vertical, shapes became more irregular, and buildings acquired decorative detail. Thomas Turner Odell, the first owner of Milton Hall, came to St Andrews at the age of fourteen to help his widowed aunt run her dry-goods business. In Odell's hands, a modest enterprise became "Manchester House," a major supplier of goods of every description. Milton Hall, built on Frederick Street in the 1860s, was meant to reflect Odell's success. Although the house was firmly and solidly built, Odell felt it was necessary to treat its plank siding (butted rather than overlapping) with a mixture of sand and paint so that it might resemble stone. A large ell (removed in the 1920s) at the back of the house contained the kitchen and, on the second floor, eight small bedrooms for the servants.

MARINE HOSPITAL

BOTTOM RIGHT

An 1822 provincial statute required vessels of sixty tons and upward entering St Andrews and other major ports to pay a duty for the upkeep of a marine hospital for the care of sick and disabled seamen. The original hospital, built in 1825, was destroyed by fire in 1872. Its replacement was built in the then popular Italianate style, modelled on the farmhouse and villa architecture of northern Italy. Characteristic features were round-headed windows, cupolas, and hipped roofs. The building is now a private residence.

MILTON HALL

MARINE HOSPITAL

Houses and Residential Streets

CAPTAIN CLARK'S HOUSE

In 1903 Captain Nelson Clark, master of the cargo schooner *Toffa*, built this elegant house on Water Street, incorporating in the structure an existing house and attaching to one end of it a "penny school" that stood on the corner of the lot. In 1921 his daughter Marjorie Richardson converted the house into a summer hotel, the Seaside Inn, which she operated until her retirement in the early 1980s. For a decade the inn lay dormant. In the 1990s, it was revived as the piquantly-named Salty Towers.

Chapter 2

Water Street

WATER STREET NEAR ITS JUNCTION WITH KING STREET

In small coastal towns around the Bay of Fundy and the Gulf of Maine, the main business street was the street closest to the shore, and it was usually named Water Street. While the Atlantic trade flourished, Water Street in St Andrews was a rich mixture of shops, inns, chandleries, boarding houses, small workshops, and warehouses. In the original town plat, the lots running down to the shore were forty feet wide, but the demand for waterfront property was such that there was further subdivision which left, in places, pencil-thin lots that were sometimes only twenty or twenty-five feet across. On the south or shore side of the street, buildings tended to be long and narrow with their gable ends facing the street. The result is a roofline that would not look out of place in some of the older port cities of Europe.

WATER STREET, LOOKING EAST

While movement was still chiefly by water and St Andrews was still a terminus for mailboats and ferries, the town served as a regional market centre. But as roads improved and automobiles became affordable, boat traffic declined and St Andrews, which had once been a hub, found itself isolated on the tip of a long peninsula. Increasingly, the town depended upon summer traffic. China, cutlery, and other fineries had long been staple imports from Europe, but Elijah Stickney was the first Maritime merchant to organize regular imports of Wedgwood and Doulton china. These became so popular throughout the Maritimes that no well-to-do bride would consider setting up house without several place settings of one or the other. In a summer resort close to the United States border, Stickney was also able to offer American visitors very attractive prices. British china entered Canada duty-free whereas American tariffs could be as high as 70 percent.

EDWIN ODELL'S DRY GOODS STORE

Across the street from Stickney's was Edwin Odell's drygoods store, housed in a fine, slate-roofed Georgian building. Edwin Odell was was the son of Thomas Turner Odell, the founder of Manchester House. In June 1930 fire gutted the store, to the delight of the town's youth but to the chagrin of the Odells, who are reported to have carried no insurance. Conditions for the fire were the classic ones for coastal towns: several dry days before the blaze and a stiff onshore breeze during it sent sparks and burning shingles onto neighbouring buildings and streets. The fire started in a disused barn behind the liquor store farther down the street and then spread to other outbuildings, finally reaching Odell's. Had the onshore breeze not subsided, the entire business section might have been destroyed. The fire carried across the street to the Stickney/Wedgwood store which was saved only by continual dousing from the attending fire brigades. Telephone poles, however, could be sacrificed and as their tops burned the wires were left dangling. The 1930 fire was the worst in the town's history and for Water Street it was a near escape.

THE NEW BRUNSWICK LIQUOR STORE

In a community that had long regarded free trade as a natural right, and where wine and spirits had been readily available, few tears would have been shed for the burning of the government liquor store. Throughout the second half of the nineteenth century, support for temperance culminated in the Scott Act of 1878, which made much of the province officially dry, and finally in Prohibition itself from 1916-1927. After 1927 the sale of all beer, wines, and spirits became a provincial government monopoly. But the shadow of Prohibition receded slowly: from 1916 until 1962 it was illegal to drink alcohol in a public place in New Brunswick.

STREET & COMPANY

BOTTOM RIGHT

Until the 1870s, J.Street & Company, which owned the building in the immediate left foreground of the photograph at right, imported beer, wines, and spirits from England, France, and the Caribbean. The back of the building overhung a wharf, allowing crates and barrels to be unloaded from the schooners and lifted directly to the upper floors of the building. London beers were ordered by the hundred dozen, and wines and spirits by the cask, the hogshead, or the pipe and offered for sale. In the 1930s the building housed a movie theatre and since the 1960s it has been a restaurant, aptly named—until it changed hands in the mid-1990s—"Smugglers Wharf." The windlass that was used to hoist barrels of wine and liquor to the upper floors decorates the dining room of the restaurant. The loft area of the restaurant is made from beams salvaged from Ordways Hall, a New England-style meeting house demolished in 1975. The Street & Company property, in its many transformations, is an example of the repeated recycling of buildings on Water Street.

WREN'S DRUG STORE

By 1900 drug stores were no longer simply drug stores. Classic victims of inelastic demand, pharmacists had to find alternatives to "Drugs, Chemicals, and Proprietary Medicines." Thomas R. Wren's answer was books, stationery, Wedgwood ware, art, china, photo supplies, and fancy goods. The figures posing nonchalantly in the photograph were members of the Algonquin band.

STREET & COMPANY

Water Street

THE KENNEDY HOTEL

Angus Kennedy, the builder of the Kennedy Hotel, was a railway contractor turned hotelier from Glengarry, Ontario. He came to St Andrews in 1857 to lay a section of the New Brunswick and Canada Railway and when his contract ran out he stayed on to buy and operate several hotels. The first two were near the railway station but the third, the Kennedy, built in 1881 on the site of the former Clarke Hotel, was in the centre of town. It was designed as a comfortable fifty-room, all-purpose hotel for both business and leisure visitors. At the back of the inn was a sample room where commercial travellers, who came by rail with large trunks, could display their wares. The hotel remained in Kennedy hands until the 1940s, at which time it was sold and became the Commodore. In the 1960s, after another change of hands, it became the Shiretown Inn, and in the 1990s the name reverted to Kennedy.

COTTAGE CRAFT

AT RIGHT

This modest shop represents the most original business in St Andrews, and the diminutive figure in front of it one of its most determined inhabitants. Grace Helen Mowat was born in St Andrews in 1875. As a young woman she studied art and design at Cooper Union in New York. She followed this education with work as an art instructor first in New York and then at a boarding school for girls in Halifax, returning to St Andrews in 1914 to look after her ageing parents. She was unmarried and had very little capital. From this unpromising platform she launched a remarkable cottage industry. A devotee of the Arts and Crafts Movement, she decided to promote a native art based on traditional rural crafts. She divided Charlotte County into districts, assigning each a forewoman to direct the work of weaving, knitting, hooking, doll-making, and embroidery. The forewoman also gave out the material, brought in the finished pieces, and paid the workers. Virtually everything was made from local wool, colours, and dyes. Motifs

GRACE HELEN MOWAT AT HER STORE ON WATER STREET

came from the everyday lives of the workers. An "art that would tell the story of the Maritimes," declared Miss Mowat, "must come from the people themselves." To workers in search of subjects, her advice was simple: "Look around you." So successful was the business that in 1924 Mowat was invited to represent Canada at the British Empire Exhibition in London. Until World War Two, Grace Helen Mowat worked from Chestnut Hall, but when the Algonquin Hotel closed during the war (depriving her of much of her clientele), she moved the retail business to a tiny store on Water Street. At the end of the war she sold the business to Kent and Bill Ross who, in 1948, moved it into an old lobster plant in Market Square. Cottage Craft now has a satellite store in that mecca for upmarket shoppers, Freeport, Maine.

BOLTS OF CLOTH

Wool for making yarn and cloth came from farms on the mainland and the islands. Deer Island wool, recalled one of the workers, was always recognizable because it tended to be full of seaweed. Washing and dyeing were the responsibility of Boyd Merrill, the dye master, chief weaver, and production manager. To get the right tones, he mixed his dyes in an iron pot. Concept and design were the domain of Grace Helen Mowat.

LORD BYNG AT CHESTNUT HALL

AT RIGHT

Lord Byng, the Governor General, visited Cottage Craft on his visit to St Andrews in July, 1923. At Chestnut Hall, the upstairs rooms were used for weaving, knitting, embroidery, and the making of handicrafts, and the basement rooms for pottery. The retail shop was on the ground floor.

LORD BYNG AT CHESTNUT HALL

NIGER REEF TEAHOUSE

Built in 1926 off the Niger Reef at the mouth of the St Croix as a chapter house for the Imperial Order of the Daughters of the Empire, this simple log structure became known as the Niger Reef Teahouse. To support the chapter's educational and welfare work, members served tea during the summer months. During World War Two the house became a workroom for the war effort and later, after a change of ownership, a rented cottage that was allowed to deteriorate. Threatened with removal or demolition in the 1990s, the building was restored by the St Andrews Civic Trust and is once again a tearoom. Also restored by the Trust were the charming murals painted by Lucille Douglas, an American who spent many years in China and who was a friend of Florence Ayscough, donor of the chapter house.

THE MALLORY HOUSE AND LIVERY STABLE

PHOTOS AT RIGHT

The building now known as the Mallory House was built for Robert Pagan, the prominent Loyalist merchant, around 1810. In 1879, after the building had served as an inn and a store, it was bought by William Mallory, a young man from a Woodstock farming family who came to St Andrews in 1876 to improve his health. Mallory won a contract to deliver mail—which then came by rail to St Andrews—to St Stephen and St George and, all local land transport being horse-drawn, he needed a livery stable. He bought the former Pagan house and barn, and although he lost the mail contract the following year, he filled the gap by ferrying passengers and baggage between the newly built Algonquin Hotel and boats and trains from Boston, Eastport, Saint John, and Montreal. He also offered sightseeing tours through scenic parts of the peninsula. By the late 1880s he needed a new and larger barn, which he opened on July 1, 1889, the beginning of the Algonquin's season.

By 1921, the year of William Mallory's death, the livery business had become a haulage and taxi service. William's son Charles, however, was a horseman rather than a mechanic and he closed the business in 1922. After 1930 the barn, with its cupola removed to improve air circulation, served as a "dry shed" for curing and storing fish for the Caribbean and West Indian markets. The barn reverted to the Mallory family in 1989 and was restored to its 1889 condition by octogenerian Harry Mallory, the grandson of William Mallory. Harry Mallory replaced the

PHOTOS OF THE MALLORY HOUSE AND LIVERY STABLE, TAKEN SEVERAL YEARS APART

cupola and, by counting the clapboards in an old photograph, replicated the original sign that hung on the barn.

    The two photographs above, taken several years apart, show the changes to the house and barn. In the top photograph, the house is restrainedly Georgian with fine, classical proportions but without any trim. Twenty or thirty years later, changes in taste and success in business have wrought notable changes. Clapboard has replaced shingles, and large-paned, double-hung windows have replaced their delicate six-paned Georgian predecessors. The house has also acquired prominent corner boards and eaves, and a substantial porch. The new barn, too, is larger and more elaborate than the old one.

THE MALLORY BUS

A taxi and haulage business needs a variety of vehicles: buses for groups and a truck for baggage and trunks, in addition to taxis for individuals. To make the truck, a local blacksmith built a frame and welded it onto the chassis of a Model T-Ford. He also adapted seats from a buckboard to fit the truck should it be needed as a bus for picnics. With the change from horse-powered to motorized transport, blacksmith shops tended to become garages for car repairs just as, in earlier days, livery stables became taxi and haulage services. At any given time in horse and buggy days there were four or five blacksmith shops in the town.

BLACKSMITH'S SHOP

TOP RIGHT

Blacksmiths and wheelwrights were to the horse and buggy era what the mechanic is to the motorized one. Wheelrights made the carts and carriages and blacksmiths shod the horses and made and repaired the iron wheel rims. This shop was probably on Queen Street, one block north of Water.

LAND COMPANY OFFICE

BOTTOM RIGHT

Across the street from the classically proportioned Mallory house is one of the few late Victorian buildings on Water Street. Spared a major fire and, as connoisseurs of architecture see it, economic growth, Water Street was scarcely touched by what is generally regarded as the least prepossessing period of Canadian architecture. As anomalous as the building is, it was a symbol of St Andrews's economic revival. In the 1880s a group of American and Canadian businessmen with railway and steamship connections floated the St Andrews Land Company. Their objective was to develop the town as a summer resort. The company bought eighty town lots as well as blocks of land in choice locations outside the old town plat. The Water Street building was the company office. It served later as the post office. It is now an apartment building.

BLACKSMITH'S SHOP

LAND COMPANY OFFICE

Water Street

Eleanor Roosevelt

Campobello and the Roosevelt summer home were less than an hour from St Andrews by power boat. James and Sara Delano Roosevelt, the parents of president Franklin D. Roosevelt, bought ten acres on Campobello in 1884 and on them built a fifteen-bedroom house. James Roosevelt was then vice-president of the Delaware and Hudson Railway. Both Franklin Delano and Eleanor Roosevelt had long associations with Campobello; Franklin was born on the island and Eleanor first visited it in 1904. The couple acquired a house on the island in 1908 and were summer visitors thereafter. There was no shopping on Campobello so Eleanor Roosevelt frequented the shops in St Andrews and Cottage Craft in particular. In the photograph at right, she is accompanied by Sir Thomas Tait, former private secretary to Sir William Van Horne and chairman of the railway commissioners of the state of Victoria, Australia.

ELEANOR ROOSEVELT AT ST ANDREWS, ACCOMPANIED BY SIR THOMAS TAIT

WOMAN WITH PONY AND TRAP

Was there ever a more elegant age for women or, for that matter, transport, than the first decade of the last century? For individuals, a pony and trap was the standard conveyance.

FIRE STATION AND THE OLD TOWN HALL, 1927

The firehall, built in 1872, was a multi-purpose building. The first floor served as a two-bay firehall, and the second as a public library and a place for town council meetings. There was no town office. The tower was necessary for draining and drying the hoses; it also housed a 426-pound warning bell that pealed the hours as well as sounded the fire alarm. A stove at the bottom of the tower hastened the drying process and, in winter, kept the hoses from freezing. Water tanks were set up in various parts of the town, but most were on Water Street, the street most vulnerable to fire. The largest tank, in Market Square, was filled with sea water and could be topped up at flood tide. In the event of a wharf or waterfront fire, water could also be pumped directly from the sea. Pumping techniques were practiced about once a month between May and October, the men running the hoses onto the town square and manning the long handles of the hand-pumpers. The usual test was to force the water over the flagstaff of the engine hall, or over the roof of the Kennedy Hotel. In 1969 the firehall was torn down but the bell has been carefully preserved on a scaffold at the back of the present town hall.

THE WINDSOR HOUSE

Windsor House, the building on the left at the corner of Water and Edward streets, was built c.1798 for Captain David Mowat and his wife Mehetible, both Loyalists. For a century it served as a family home but in 1895, after a major renovation by William Morrison, the former residence became the Morrison Hotel and, as a corollary, the local stage coach stop. In 1903, after another change of hands, the hotel acquired its present name, the Windsor House. But in the course of the last century the building deteriorated markedly. Part residence, boarding house, and apartment building, its rooms were subdivided and its surfaces covered and re-covered. In the 1990s, both the interior and the exterior of the building were painstakingly restored and refurbished and, operating once again as the Windsor House, it is now an elegant hotel.

J. ROSS, SHOEMAKER

AT RIGHT

At the time of this photograph Jim Ross was a cobbler, a repairer rather than a maker of shoes. Yet the sign points to a time, before mass manufacture and marketing, when the chief providers of everyday goods were artisans who both made and sold the product on their premises. Bakers, tinsmiths, saddlers, tanners, and tailors all belonged to this category. Jim Ross also repaired harnesses for the local livery stables.

J. ROSS, SHOEMAKER

Water Street

THE OLD COFFEE HOUSE

Coffee houses, in which issues great and small were debated daily, were an essential adjunct to political and social life in eighteenth-century towns. The St Andrews coffee house first served the inhabitants of Castine and was dismantled and transported at the time of the evacuation. It was reassembled on William Street, just below Water, and burned in the 1930 fire.

Chapter 3

The Waterfront

DOONE'S FISH WHARF AND FACTORY

In this complex of buildings, fish were gutted, cleaned, dried, smoked, and salted. The two large, gable-roofed buildings were for smoking herring, haddock, and salmon. Herring, threaded onto sticks and hung high above smouldering sawdust fires, were smoked in the building nearest the end of the wharf. Boxes and barrels were made in the small building, the cooper's shed, at the end of the wharf. The gabled building at the head of the wharf was a drying shed for cod, haddock, and pollock. Dried fish for the American and West Indian markets went by boat to Eastport and Boston, and from Boston to the West Indies. Doone's business never recovered from the collapse of the West Indian market during the Great Depression and it closed in the 1940s. The wharf, like most of its neighbours on the waterfront, succumbed to neglect, rot, and winter ice. In 1949 the herring smoke-house is said to have blown "clear across to Robbinston (Maine)."

THE SHORELINE, LOOKING EAST

In the early days of European settlement, the sea was both a highway and a vital resource that was exploited by New England fishermen long before the arrival of the Loyalists. There was some cultivable land along the St Croix, but for the most part the soils of the peninsula were too rough to farm. But if the land was unproductive, the sea was bountiful. The turbulent, nutrient-rich waters of Passamaquoddy and the Bay of Fundy supported large populations of herring, hake, haddock, and pollock as well as clams, scallops, and lobsters. Passamaquoddy is an Indian word meaning "the bay where the pollock are." Seasonally, too, the St Croix was plugged with salmon, gaspereau, shad, and striped bass, so much so that at the falls in St Stephen they could, during runs, be hand-dipped into barrels. In May, herring were sometimes so numerous near the mouth of the St Croix that they could be taken with scoop nets attached to long poles.

ROCK PICKING AT O'NEILL'S FARM

TOP RIGHT

The St Andrews peninsula, like so many parts of the Maritimes, was a land of hard-scrabble farming where there was enough fieldstone to wall the fields. O'Neill's farm is just outside the town on the southeastern side of the peninsula. Several of the fields remain open but the farmhouse and the barn have gone and the land is no longer worked. In the background is Minister's Island.

CHAMCOOK WEIR

BOTTOM RIGHT

Fish were taken in a number of ways but the most ingenious method was the trap, or weir, for catching herring, the most numerous of the fish. A Mi'kmaq invention, the weir is a long, sinuous arrangement of poles and woven brush or nets built along coastlines and headlands where herring were known to run. The long wings of the weir guided the herring into circular enclosures that, by curling in on themselves, trapped the fish. The poles—usually birch saplings—were driven into the mud or, if the bottom was hard, anchored with rocks. To prevent the escape of the herring the poles were at first interlaced with brush and hung with netting. Chamcook is a coastal village about three miles from St Andrews.

ROCK PICKING AT O'NEILL'S FARM

CHAMCOOK WEIR

Seining a Weir ABOVE

Fish caught in the brush weirs were ladled or dip-netted into boats at low or ebb tide. If the water was low enough the fish could even be loaded directly into carts. With net weirs, the nets were hauled or "seined" in and the herring dumped into boats. Impounding the herring and cutting off their food supply ensured that the fish were clean when harvested. Herring caught by purse seiners out at sea, on the other hand, were usually "feedy."

Loading herring into a carrier LEFT

To remove the scales before the herring were delivered to the canneries, men in oiled trousers with boots tied tight scuffed backward and forward among the fish without lifting their feet from the bottom of the boat. Today herring scales are manufactured into guanine or pearl essence, an iridescent material that, among other uses, adds gloss to lipstick and sheen to costume jewelry.

Sardine cannery, Chamcook

Until the invention of tin canning in the 1860s there was no market for small herring, or sardines. Larger herring could be salted, dried, smoked, and marketed whole in the West Indies or as fillets in the American bar trade. At first, the chief clearing houses for Passamaquoddy fish were the Maine ports of Eastport and Lubec. But the turn of the nineteenth century saw the development of Canadian canneries, the largest and most ambitious of which was the Canadian Sardine

Company (Cansarco) in Chamcook, a few miles from St Andrews. Underwritten in 1911 by a group of financiers—among them Sir William Van Horne and Lord Shaughnessy—with St Andrews and CPR connections, Cansarco was to be an all-purpose factory for canning vegetables, fruit, clams, and scallops as well as sardines. When operating, it would employ many hundreds of workers who were to be the nucleus of a model community, St Andrews North, served by a bank, grocery and department stores, a movie theatre, billiard and pool rooms, and a shuttle bus to St Andrews. The plant and a fleet of sardine carriers were built and workers were hired. But there was trouble even before production began. In May 1912 a strike by Italian construction workers led to the deportation of the "ringleader," and in December 1912 twenty plant workers were laid off for insubordination. There were reports of liquor being sold outside the compound and of such disorder within that a lock-up had to be built for the unruly. Production began in March 1913, but gross mismanagement and misspending had so emptied company coffers that the banks withdrew their support. Work was suspended in August 1913 and all three hundred employees were laid off. The final ignominy came a year later when the plant was sold to the Bank of Nova Scotia at a public auction at the Kennedy Hotel in St Andrews, reportedly for a knock-down price. The plant never re-opened.

BOARDING HOUSES, CHAMCOOK

To operate the plant, experienced workers had to be brought in and housing had to be provided: cottages for the married workers and dormitories and boarding houses, with central dining and recreation rooms, for the unmarried. Among the imported workers were a hundred Norwegian girls who arrived several weeks before the dormitories were ready. To house the girls, the company leased a clam factory in St Andrews and converted the two upper floors into sleeping quarters. The lower floor became a dining room and kitchen. Heat for the building and for cooking came from a steam boiler and a steam cooker used for processing the clams.

COD FLAKES DRYING AT DOONE'S WHARF

TOP RIGHT

Before refrigeration and the railway, fish bound for distant markets had to be salted, then pickled, canned, or smoked. When landed, ground fish such as cod and pollock were split, gutted, lightly salted, and wind dried on open wooden platforms or "flakes." For market, the fish were barreled, the choice cod going to Boston and New York and the best pollock to the lumber camps of Maine and New Brunswick. Fish of inferior quality usually ended up in the West Indies. Because of its poor salting qualities relative to cod and pollock, the now-prized haddock was of much less commercial importance. As the ferry in the background indicates, the taste for dried and salted fish survived the coming of the steamship and the railway.

BRINGING IN THE CATCH

BOTTOM RIGHT

The common practice among fish processors was to engage a buyer to collect the catch from the fishermen and deliver it to the processing plant for cleaning and gutting and, if necessary, salting and drying.

COD FLAKES DRYING AT DOONE'S WHARF

BRINGING IN THE CATCH

The Waterfront

GREENLAW'S FISH FACTORY

GREENLAW'S FISH FACTORY

LEFT

Dried cod was shipped in barrels or drums made from kiln-dried wood to reduce the possibility of moisture from the wood contaminating the fish. The fish were packed in layers, head to tail, and rammed tight with a pole until the barrel was full and of the right weight. A screw jack pressed the lid into place and nails held it shut. Bloaters and fresh fish were packed more gently in boxes weighing up to thirty pounds, and fresh fish were packed in ice. The large, trophy-sized fish in the photograph at left is a halibut. To the right is a freshwater tank for cleaning the fish.

CONLEY'S LOBSTER PLANT

ABOVE

In the early days of settlement, lobsters were supposedly so plentiful that they could be picked up at low water or taken from a boat with a gaffe—a cod hook with the barb removed—or even a forked stick. Folk memory also has it that after a storm, when windrows of them might be piled on the beaches, lobsters were hauled onto the fields to be used as fertilizer. Until the arrival of the motorized truck and the train, the only answer to marketing lobsters was to pack them in hermetically sealed containers. By the mid-1860s there were small lobster canneries in St Andrews, Grand Manan, and Eastport.

Ed Conley, the figure in the foreground, shipped live lobsters to Boston from his plant on the market wharf at St Andrews. He used the trucks to bring lobsters from Shediac, on the Northumberland Strait, during the closed season at St Andrews. The lobsters were moved overnight, when temperatures were low, and on arrival were transferred to large, partly submerged crates, or "cars," that were anchored in the harbour beside the plant. They were later shipped to Boston. To solve the problems posed by a seasonal fishery, Conley built a lobster pound—the first in the Maritimes—on Deer Island; the pound was fed year-round by cold, tidal water. In 1944/45 Ed Conley opened a new plant at North Point farther along the St Andrews shore. The old plant became the new home of Cottage Craft.

A MOVEABLE MARINE BIOLOGICAL STATION

The prolific, nutrient-rich waters of Passamaquoddy Bay were as attractive to marine biologists as they were to fishermen. Recognizing that study of the marine life of the bay could be invaluable to the fishery, in 1893 Canada's Commissioner and Inspector of Fisheries expressed the need for a marine biological station. The government's response was a fifty-foot-long portable laboratory, similar in shape to a Pullman car, that lay beached above high water at Indian Point, St Andrews. In 1901 the laboratory was loaded onto a scow and towed to locations in Nova Scotia, Prince Edward Island, and finally the Gaspé Peninsula where it was wrecked while being towed to Sept Isles on the north shore of the St Lawrence.

A PERMAMENT MARINE BIOLOGICAL STATION

BELOW

When, in 1907, the federal government acknowledged the need for a permanent fisheries research station, St Andrews was almost automatically the choice for its location. No other Maritime port could offer the same combination of advantages. St Andrews's chief rival was Chester in Nova Scotia, but the Nova Scotia fleets fished for the most part off the Grand Banks, and the catches went directly to the Boston market, or, if the catches were brought home, they were already barreled

for shipment. To a local fishery that offered weirs from which material could easily be collected, sheltered waters of varying depths, and flora and fauna of remarkable richness, St Andrews could add excellent rail connections to Boston and Montreal and the amenities of an historic town and a fashionable resort. Until 1928 most of the researchers came from eastern universities and—having other winter responsibilities—in summer only. Since 1928, when federal government scientists began replacing professors, research has been conducted year-round.

LIBRARY AND ATTIC IN THE OLD LABORATORY

Both were destroyed by fire in 1932.

The Waterfront

REPAIRING LOBSTER TRAPS

Dr. J. Stafford, marine biologist, and his assistant A.E. Calder.

RAILWAY TRESTLE

TOP RIGHT

To restore the town's economy after the loss of the Atlantic and the West Indies trade in the 1830s and 1840s, a group of St Andrews businessmen proposed to make St Andrews the winter port of Canada by building a railway to Quebec City. The St Andrews-Quebec route was, in fact, the shortest route between the Atlantic and the St Lawrence. Funds were raised but a dispute between Britain and the United States over territory that was later ceded to Maine interrupted building and the projected line was never completed. By the time the border dispute was settled, both Halifax and Saint John had decided that they, too, would make excellent winter ports. The St Andrews line was later absorbed by the CPR system. Although St Andrews never became the winter port, the line was used for transporting lumber and potatoes from the interior and fish from St Andrews. In St Andrews itself a trestle ran along the waterfront, linking the wharves.

HULKS AND ROTTING WHARVES

BOTTOM RIGHT

By the 1880s and 1890s, the date of these photographs, shipping was almost at a standstill and hulks and decaying wharves lined the shore. Pleasure boats would eventually enliven the harbour, but the wharves rotted away. A waterfront once served by a dozen wharves now has only one.

RAILWAY TRESTLE

HULKS AND ROTTING WHARVES

The Waterfront

COAL-CARRYING SCHOONERS

By the end of the nineteenth century the Treat & Foster building that had once been a warehouse for French claret, Dutch gin, Spanish port, and London beer had been reduced to handling coal. Imported by the Quoddy Coal Company, coal was one of the few sea-borne commodities still brought to St Andrews and these shipments, too, would end when oil replaced coal as heating fuel. Soft coals came from the United States and the more valuable hard coals from Wales and Scotland.

THE *ROSE STANDISH* AT THE STEAMBOAT OR PENDLEBURY WHARF

BOTTOM RIGHT

Until the 1930s and 1940s there were regular passenger, freight, and mail services from St Andrews up the St Croix to Calais and St Stephen and to the neighbouring islands. But as roads improved and automobiles became more commonplace, ferry services were cancelled or, in the case of the island services, the mainland termini were moved to locations more convenient than St Andrews. This photograph, taken in 1889, shows passengers waiting to board the sidewheel steamer the *Rose Standish*. Built in Brooklyn in 1863, the *Rose Standish* ran between Calais and Easport for the Frontier Steamboat Company of Calais. At Eastport, passengers could transfer to boats for Portland, Boston, and Saint John. This photograph shows the *Rose Standish* in its last season of operation; while being readied for the 1890 season, the vessel caught fire and burned at its mooring in Calais.

Captain of the *Grand Manan*

The ferry to Grand Manan was St Andrews's last vital sea link to the islands. The service ended in the 1960s.

THE *ROSE STANDISH* AT THE PENDLEBURY WHARF

HOIST ON THE MARKET WHARF

RIGHT

Fish and freight were lifted onto the town wharf by this simple yet effective arrangement of wheels and cogs.

PENDLEBURY LIGHT

BELOW

Built in 1833, the Pendlebury Light guided vessels into the St Andrews harbour for more than a century. The first keeper, John Pendlebury, who was the son of a blacksmith at the naval yard in New York, came to St Andrews in 1785 aboard a sloop owned by Robert Pagan. Pendleburys manned the lighthouse until it was replaced in 1938 by an electric pole light fixed to the end of the CPR wharf. The lighthouse building is now a restaurant. In this photograph the CPR loading wharf is to the left of the lighthouse, but by 1890, as the figures on the beach suggest, summer visitors were beginning to replace freight as cargo.

Chapter 4

Men in Uniform

READY FOR WAR!

In St Andrews, as elsewhere in the British Dominions, the beginning of World War One was an occasion for unrestrained expressions of patriotism. At a recruiting rally for the 26th Battalion in November 1914, both church and state called young men to the colours. Captain Elliott, recruiting officer for the battalion, brought a message "direct from his Majesty the King" urging young men to fight for the "liberty, honour and integrity of the empire." The town's clergy claimed an even higher authority: God and the Right were on England's side. In what was described as a forcible speech, the Anglican rector counseled young women, wives, and mothers "not to throw any sentimental obstacles" in their way. By the end of November 1914, St Andrews, with a population of just over a thousand, had delivered thirty of its young men. Only their extreme youth would have kept these eager young cadets in the photograph from serving at the front. For boys younger than these, Eaton's made tailored military uniforms so that they might ape their fathers and older brothers.

THREE MILITARY GENTLEMEN

For the first half of the nineteenth century, uniformed men were a common sight in St Andrews. Relations between Great Britain and the United States, inevitably strained after the Revolution, deteriorated markedly after the latter supported the French during the Napoleonic Wars (1793-1815). But once the threat of invasion by the Americans had passed, St Andrews's strategic importance declined rapidly. For British regulars who were garrisoned in the town until 1866, St Andrews was not an onerous posting and, for officers, it was a socially agreeable one.

WEST POINT BLOCKHOUSE

The danger to St Andrews came not from neighbours across the river but from privateers and marauders from states farther south. Realizing that the town was practically defenceless, the townspeople built two crude shore batteries commanding the eastern and western entrances to the harbour. On the advice of a British field officer, during the winter of 1812/13 blockhouses were built behind each battery to back up the guns and prevent their capture. The officer also advocated a third blockhouse, at Joe's Point, to guard the mouth of the St Croix River. The military appointed an engineer officer to supervise the construction of these blockhouses but refused to pay for either materials or labour on the grounds that they were being built to protect private property. Robert Pagan and Christopher Scott, a Scottish merchant, banker, and shipbuilder, solicited subscriptions from the community but in the end the town's merchants seem to have footed the bill, Scott himself donating 175 pounds. After the war, the British, who obviously placed a low value on the strategic importance of St Andrews, decided it was too costly to maintain a full complement of troops and allowed two of the blockhouses to decay. The survivor, the middle or West Point blockhouse, they manned with a small detachment of Royal Artillery who used it as a barracks. The militia, the principal defenders of the town, kept their arms in the upper store.

The blockhouses were made of twelve-inch-squared wall timbers, dovetailed at the corners and chinked. Round-log walls were weak along the joints, allowing musket balls to penetrate and send wood splinters tearing through the interior.

In addition to gunports and loopholes, openings were cut in the floor of the overhang to cover attackers directly below.

A MOTHBALLED BLOCKHOUSE

Apart from military alerts in the Aroostook War (1838-42) and the Fenian threat of 1866, when the guns were remounted but never fired, the West Point blockhouse was mothballed. After 1835 it was leased as a residence to retired artillerymen for a shilling a month, plus the care of the grounds. The property passed to the Canadian government in 1867 following the confederation of the provinces, but civilian occupation continued until the 1960s when the blockhouse was designated a national historic site and restored to its early nineteeth century condition. In the summer of 1993 fire destroyed the roof and second floor of the building but the original walls survived. A complete restoration began in the spring of 1994.

ONE OF THE 24-POUNDERS

TOP RIGHT

One of the six 24-pound guns that made up the battery at the West Point blockhouse.

FORT TIPPERARY, 1890

BOTTOM RIGHT

While the blockhouses commanded the harbour and the western approaches to the town, the eastern or Katy's Cove approach lay beneath the guns of Fort Tipperary, built in 1814/15 on a height of land above the town. The twelve-acre site formerly belonged to the Anglican Church and was exchanged for adjacent government reservation land, presumably to give the fort a more commanding position. Like the blockhouses, the fort was made of large squared timbers, in this case hewn pine logs eleven inches thick, that were portholed to repel advancing invaders. It seems to have been garrisoned until after the Fenian threat in 1866, then abandoned. By July 1840 the building was the worse for wear; the *St Andrews Standard* disparaged it as an "unsightly and antiquated erection...miserably adapted for the comfort and convenience of its gallant occupants." In 1902, when the buildings were removed to make room for a summer home for Lord Shaughnessy, president of the CPR, the *Standard's* successor, the *Beacon*, took a different view. The fort was now a doughty old warrior that had "braved the battle and the breeze for eighty and more years." This photograph shows the main barrack building, the officers' quarters, a guardhouse, and a sergeant's cottage.

ONE OF THE 24-POUNDERS

FORT TIPPERARY. 1890

Men in Uniform

St Andrews Rifle Company, 1861-65

For want of sufficient regular troops, the defence of the town depended largely on its militia, increasingly so as British and US relations improved and St Andrews's strategic importance declined. In general, the provincial militias were not impressive military forces. They were organized on a county and local basis, each unit drawing its officers and men from the vicinity. Because all men between the ages of sixteen and sixty were eligible, the militias were invariably an assortment of tradesmen, farmers, labourers, lumbermen, former soldiers, and raw youths. They seldom had enough arms and equipment and their commanders tended to be ageing veterans. Discipline was seldom what it should have been. When Colonel Joseph Gubbins of the English regular army inspected the St Andrews Militia in 1811, he remarked that they were "a fine body of men but in a bad state as a battalion, the officers having been recommended for their appointments by the Lieutenant Colonel without any regard to their qualifications as military persons. In this district, as well as in several others, making a strong party for the next election of [government] representatives is more considered than the defence of the province."

Militia at ease in front of the Clarke Hotel, c.1860   TOP RIGHT

Militia on parade, c.1860

BOTTOM RIGHT

Militias were subject to regular drills and inspections which were conducted in St Andrews in or near the market square. Before it was destroyed by fire in the 1870s, the building directly behind the assembled militiamen had various uses and was known by various names, most commonly in later times as the Market House. Earlier it had been a gaol and a courthouse. The gaol, which was simply two large rooms, was on the ground floor. After a new gaol and courthouse were built, the ground floor became a meat market and the second floor a town hall and armoury. The building was also a place of execution; early in the nineteenth century a black brother and sister were hanged from a crossbeam for the crime of infanticide.

MILITIA AT EASE IN FRONT OF THE CLARKE HOTEL, C.1860

MILITIA ON PARADE, C.1860

THE WOODSTOCK FIELD BATTERY

SUMMER CAMP, 1889

PHOTOS ABOVE AND BELOW

With good rail connections and open, common lands on each side of the town, St Andrews was an ideal location for military camps. In July 1889 infantry, cavalry, and engineers from the 67th and 71st Battalions and the Princess Louise Hussars assembled in St Andrews and camped for ten days at Joe's Point. These photographs were taken on the afternoon of Dominion Day when the troops paraded on open ground near the camp tents and performed manoeuvres and exercises for the many spectators. One exercise involved a mock attack on Fort Tipperary.

SOLDIERS ON PARADE

DEPARTURE OF THE VOLUNTEERS

PHOTOS BELOW

To prepare for the departure of the volunteers, a meeting, chaired by the mayor, convened at the Kennedy Hotel. It was agreed that the St Andrews Brass Band would head the procession followed by boys from the public schools bearing flags. The mayor and council, the school trustees, male citizens, and "soldier boys" would follow on foot. The mayor agreed to ask all merchants to close their doors at four o'clock so that every citizen might attend the parade. A special committee would organize the raising of flags and the floating of bunting. The result of the mayor's initiative was a half-mile-long procession that marched, to prolonged cheering from bystanders, from the Kennedy Hotel to the railway station.

Men in Uniform

WIVES, GIRLFRIENDS, PARENTS, AND FAMILY MEMBERS VISITED BEFORE EMBARKATION

VISITING DAY AT THE CAMP OF THE 4TH OVERSEAS PIONEER BATTALION

In late May 1916, five hundred men of the 4th Pioneers, drawn from depots across the country, assembled in St Andrews to prepare for embarkation overseas. Before leaving, one of the companies had to be brought up to strength from 120 men to the required 250. In Saint John, St Stephen, and St Andrews, recruiting officers looked for construction men, blacksmiths, bridge workers, railway construction workers, and lumbermen who could build roads, bridges, and entrenchments at or near the front. Foremen were especially valued and were promised positions as non-commissioned officers. Every officer in the battalion was either an engineer or a contractor accustomed to construction work. Recruits were also sought for the 4th Pioneers' brass band, whose instruments had been donated by an Ottawa construction company. Lumbermen who enlisted were allowed to finish their work on the spring drives.

VISITING BEFORE EMBARKATION

AT LEFT

Wives, girlfriends, parents and family members visited the camp before embarkation. The mood was festive despite the enormous casualties in France. Behind the lone soldier in the photograph at left is the blockhouse built for a war that, in New Brunswick at least, shed no blood.

CAPTURED GERMAN GUN This gun was a trophy from the World War One, brought to St Andrews and mounted on a cement base at Indian Point by the local branch of the Royal Canadian Legion. Until they were moved to Market Square in 1925, Armistice Day services were held at Indian Point around the gun. It was removed from its base and hauled away around 1940 as scrap metal for the new war effort—World War Two.

CAVALRYMEN AT THE 1916 CAMP

PRIVATE VINCENT MCQUOID

Of three McQuoid brothers to enlist in World War One, Vincent was the only survivor. Charles (21), of the 26th Battalion, was killed in action in 1916; Fraser (20), of the 115th Battalion, died in a military hospital a year later, in July 1917. In his last letter home, Charles McQuoid wrote: "We came out of the trenches a few days ago. This is an awful warm day—am sweating to beat the band…The farmers over here have started their haying; it won't be long till they are at it over there. The time soon flies. I was on the ocean this time last year, drawing near the Straits of Dover, one of the prettiest scenes I ever saw—the white cliffs and blue water." World War One claimed the lives of twenty-nine St Andrews men.

Men in Uniform

A CALL TO ARMS, 1940 By 1940, St Andrews and the entire Western world had lost its appetite for war. In spite of a rousing speech in May 1940 by King George VI calling for "courage and purpose," the official Call to Arms, read from the steps of the post office, is witnessed only by the squad of attending soldiers, a handful of schoolchildren, and a few passing pedestrians.

Chapter 5

Churches, Schools, and Public Buildings

CHAPEL OF EASE OF SAINT JOHN THE BAPTIST, CHAMCOOK

Early in the nineteenth century a small group of English families settled around the Chamcook estuary, about three miles from St Andrews. They cleared land for farming and built grist mills, saw mills, and shipyards. The most prominent of the men, John Wilson, built a large brick house, "Forest Lodge," in a beech wood that he stocked with deer in an effort to create an English park. To make an English village of the Chamcook settlement, in the early 1840s he and neighbour John Townsend donated land for a church and subscribed liberally to a general building fund. The chapel, built from local sandstone, is a corner of England on a foreign shore. Bishop Medley, who consecrated the chapel, described it as "beautifully situated on a piece of ground beneath a high wooded hill, overlooking one of the numerous creeks with which that part of the country abounds."

ALL SAINTS CHURCH

The town's first Anglican church was a small building near the junction of King and Water streets that—as the only church to receive government support—for many years served Protestants of all denominations. In 1855, the Anglican congregation established a building fund for a new church and in 1866 it was able to begin building at the junction of King and Montague. The original plan, prepared by a Boston church architect, called for a stone building in the then popular Perpendicular or Gothic style, but the costs of such a project quickly had the vestry searching for alternatives. The compromise was to retain the architect's overall plan but to substitute a Norman tower for a spire and New Brunswick spruce and pine for stone. Inside the church hang British and New Brunswick flags and inscribed in the central window is the unequivocal motto: Fear God and Honour the King. But the most potent symbol of allegiance hangs in the west portal: a wood carving of the coat of arms of William and Mary (1688-1694) presented to the church at Wallingford in the once-loyal province of Connecticut and brought to St Andrews in 1786 or 1787. The surrounding fence in this photograph has been removed and the church now stands in a splendid greensward.

GREENOCK CHURCH

RIGHT

The unified Protestant community did not long survive the death in 1818 of the first Anglican rector, the latitudinarian Samuel Andrews. His successor, J.H. Mercer, was an authoritarian who insisted that the last word in all church affairs lay with the rector. Disgruntled, the Presbyterians began to move away, conducting services in nearby Ordways Hall until they were able to build a church of their own. They began construction in 1821, but with the building only partially shingled they ran out of funds and the building stood unfinished. However, after hearing an Anglican denunciation of the ineffectualness of the Presbyterians, an indignant Christopher Scott completed the building in 1824 from his own funds, finishing both the shingling and the interior. Relations between the mercurial Scott and his fellow Presbyterians, however, were not always smooth and on one occasion he is said to have locked them out of the church. Whatever the ecclesiastical consequences of the Presbyterians' break with the Anglicans, the architectural ones were a blessing. Greenock is a beautifully proportioned Wren-style church featuring a pedimented doorway, palladian windows, and an octagonal belfry and spire.

GREENOCK CHURCH

67 Churches, Schools, and Public Buildings

LOYALIST BURYING GROUND

The Loyalist burying ground is on land given to the town by Jeremiah Pote. Sadly, one of the first stones to be erected commemorated his twenty-five-year-old son Robert who died of fever at sea when returning from Jamaica. Jeremiah Pote did not long survive his son; he died two years later. Although Pote was an Anglican, the cemetery was open to all denominations until the other churches could establish their own graveyards. Burials within the town limits were allowed until 1867. Although fenced in 1905, the Loyalist cemetery was largely neglected until 1981/1982 when the St Andrews Civic Trust undertook the cleaning and repairing of the stones.

THE CHURCH OF ST ANDREW

BOTTOM RIGHT

In 1815 at the end of the Napoleonic Wars, Irish emigrants began to arrive in St Andrews in large numbers. In the peak years of emigration, between 1818 and 1820, as many as four thousand might have landed, and as many as ten thousand before the Famine years 1846-1849. Most moved on to the United States or to other parts of the province, but from among those who remained in or near St Andrews were enough Roman Catholics to warrant the building of a church. The trustees were named in 1820, and in 1824 construction was started, the trustees having undertaken "within a space of eleven days…[and] in a good and workmanlike manner, [to] frame and raise a certain building, intended for a Chapel." They also undertook to assemble whatever materials might be needed and such rum and refreshments as the builders might require. (A daily supply of rum was more often than not taken for granted in the hiring.) By 1851 just over fifty percent of the heads of households in St Andrews were Irish-born. The first Roman Catholic church was built on Parr Street at its junction with Mary Street. In this photograph, taken about 1890, the view is westward, toward Joe's Point.

UNITED BAPTIST CHURCH

ABOVE

The first United Baptist church in the district, at Bayside on the St Croix Rive about four miles above St Andrews, dates from about 1840. At an 1838 meeting, the Baptist Association also determined to build a second church in St Andrews, but not until 1865, with the raising of a church on King Street, was its ambition realized. Where the Bayside church is of classical design—a rectangular building with a gable roof and a well-proportioned door and windows—the St Andrews church (above) was built in the remarkable Carpenter Gothic style. The church's graceful ornamental spires and pointed-arch door and windows were built not from stone, the customary building material in Europe, but from wood. The name of the builder has been lost.

THE CHURCH OF ST. ANDREW

The Second Church of St Andrew

By the last quarter of the nineteenth century the Roman Catholic population had outgrown the capacity of its first church. A replacement church in the popular Gothic style was built on King Street in 1885/86.

WESLEYAN UNITED CHURCH

By 1830, Methodism had a strong enough presence in St Andrews for the town to be declared a Methodist station. The first missionary, Englishman Henry Daniel, who had to preach in a borrowed or a rented hall, urged the building of a chapel that would discourage the promiscuous mixing of rich and poor that had been impossible to prevent in the hall. A small (36ft x 41ft) chapel with classical lines was boarded in by November 1831 and finished in 1832. In the spring of 1864 the decision to build a larger church on the site of the original chapel forced the removal of the chapel to an adjoining lot. A feature of the new church that caught the attention of the *St Andrews Standard* on its inaugural Sunday in the spring of 1867 was the semi-circular pews, roomy and easy to sit in, a great improvement on the old-style, stiff "box" pews.

THE ST ANDREWS GRAMMAR SCHOOL

Until 1871 there was no system of community or tax-supported schools. The town's first secondary school, created by an act of the provincial legislature in 1816, operated under the aegis of the Anglican Church. It received some government support. The Anglican rector was the president of the board and the remaining directors were all prominent Loyalists. The original building, square and hip-roofed, had a bell tower and a main classroom dominated by a pulpit-like structure from which the master declaimed and also listened to translations from Greek and Latin. Later, the building was enlarged, acquiring a gable roof and the simple, elegant proportions demonstrated in this photograph by A.A. Shirley. It stood at the upper end of King Street but in 1910 it was moved to a lot farther down the street to make way for the new Prince Arthur School. The old grammar school ended its days ignominiously as a storage shed behind a Water Street grocery store. It was destroyed in the fire of 1930. In the background is Linden Grange, built in 1829 and purchased for use as a summer residence in 1871 by Sir Leonard Tilley, one of the Fathers of Confederation and two-time Lieutenant Governor of New Brunswick.

CLASSROOM IN THE OLD GRAMMAR SCHOOL

The school's original mandate was to teach Latin, Greek, orthography, the use of globes, and practical mathematics to the sons of Loyalists. Not until 1868 was it opened to daughters and not until 1871, under the Free

School Act, did it become part of the free school system of the province. Its name was then changed to Charlotte County Grammar School.

THE FIRST ELEMENTARY SCHOOL

BELOW

Nineteenth-century elementary education seems to have been haphazard and, for the poor, inadequate. The only free schools were the Church-organized Madras schools that operated on a distinctive hand-me-down principle. The masters taught the monitors and the monitors taught the classes and corrected the exercises. The first of these "monitorial schools" dates from 1820, and the first purpose-built Madras school from 1839. By 1863 it had forty to fifty pupils. Rooms in private houses were also used as classrooms; the householders—most of whom were not qualified as teachers—offered elementary schooling for a penny a week. They were known as "penny schools." Provincial surveys in 1844 and 1868 revealed that much of the schooling in the parish and the county was conducted in rooms, and sometimes sheds, which had neither blackboards, desks, or tables. In most districts there was no substantial change until the Free Schools Act of 1871.

This photograph is of St Andrews's first elementary school. In 1867 the Parish School Committee bought the former Methodist chapel that had been moved to make way for the new church and was then being used for meetings and for the Sunday school. For the next forty years the chapel at the junction of William and Montague streets served as the St Andrews Elementary School.

INTERMEDIATE SCHOOL

Like the elementary school, the intermediate school was also makeshift. The building it occupied was first a warehouse, then a customs building. In 1870 the building was moved to the corner of William and Carleton streets and, with the addition of a bell tower, it became a school. This photograph dates from 1880. With the opening of a new comprehensive school in 1912, the building was expendable once again. The ell was removed and the main building was moved to Parr Street near its junction with Elizabeth, where it was converted into an apartment building still in use today. Through the use of skids and winches, wooden buildings could be, and were, moved around at will.

PRINCE ARTHUR SCHOOL

PHOTOS AT RIGHT

Prince Arthur School, completed in 1912, was a comprehensive school that could accommodate all grades. It supplanted all existing schools. The grammar school, whose site it occupied, was moved aside; it served as a boarding house for the builders of the new school. The second photograph, bottom right, is of the dedication ceremony in August 1912, attended by Governor General the Duke of Connaught—after whom the school was named—and Sir William and Lady Van Horne.

PRINCE ARTHUR SCHOOL

THE DEDICATION CEREMONY FOR PRINCE ARTHUR SCHOOL, 1912

Churches, Schools, and Public Buildings

LEARNING THE LESSONS

All grades were taught at Prince Arthur School and the classes were mixed, although girls and boys used separate entrances. Both photographs were taken in 1925, an era of open-topped wooden desks, inkwells, and scratchy, steel-nibbed pens. Instruction then stressed the three Rs and the geography and history of the Empire. Grades nine, ten, and eleven occupied the same classroom. The inkwells of the older boys were reportedly sometimes filled with rum or gin. Prince Arthur School closed in 1966.

CHARLOTTE COUNTY GAOL

The original gaol consisted of two large, ground-floor rooms in the Market Hall building on Water Street. The rooms were damp and, in a rowdy seaport, subject to overcrowding. In a petition to the legislature, the town complained of an "immense number" of criminals and of the inconvenience of having a courthouse in the same building. The issue that had "long been a matter of public notoriety" was settled in 1831 when a new site, an open square a few streets back from the crowded waterfront, was chosen for both a gaol and a courthouse. Because safe incarceration was the more urgent problem, the gaol was built first, in 1832, from massive granite blocks shipped by scow from a quarry in Deer Isle, Maine. Despite the thickness of the walls there were gaol-breaks, the most dramatic performed by two slim youths charged in 1861 with stealing boots and shoes from a store in Calais. They "ingeniously" slid back the bolts to the doors of their cells—which had not been padlocked—cut through a one-and-a-half inch thick iron bar in the hallway window, and squeezed through the narrow opening. The last inmates were removed in 1975, and since 1982 the building has been the home of the Charlotte County Archives. The ground floor prisoners block, however, with its heavy steel doors and dark, cave-like cells, remains untouched, a reminder to contemporary visitors of the heavy-handedness of nineteenth-century justice. Prisoners subsisted on a diet of bread and tea and, on Saturday nights, a hot meal of beans, beef stew, or fish soup. They slept on straw-filled palettes. The gaol was also a place of execution, the last of which was conducted in 1945 in a yard at the back of the building.

CHARLOTTE COUNTY COURTHOUSE

One of the stipulations for the new courthouse was that it be "more elevated," the old site having been condemned as "low and unhealthy." In a culture that equated height with authority, justice could now be dispensed from on high. The new courthouse and gaol stand on an old shoreline many feet above Water Street. To emphasize the classical form and structural solidity of the building, architect Thomas Berry added heavy pilasters of seasoned pine on each of the four exterior corners and on each side of the substantial double doors. This photograph, taken in 1912, is a reminder that the courthouse was much more than a place for dispensing justice. The crowd in this case has assembled to witness the nomination of the candidates for the 1911 "Reciprocity" election.

ORDWAYS HALL

Built in 1810, Ordways Hall was one of several New England style meeting halls in the Maritimes. Although designed as a place for community events, it was variously a hotel, an apartment house, a temporary courthouse, a ballroom, and the headquarters of the Knights of Pythias. It was demolished in 1975 to make room for a parking lot. Ordways Hall was the only remaining example of a New England style meeting hall in the Maritimes. The carrying beams were hand-hewn "two by tens" with doweled ends; even the roof rafters were of an unusual weight and configuration. From its ruins emerged the St Andrews Civic Trust.

Chapter 6

Bands and Parades

THE ARRIVAL OF THE DUKE OF CONNAUGHT, 1912

The dedication of the new Prince Arthur School in August 1912 virtually guaranteed a vice-regal visit. His Royal Highness Prince Arthur, Duke of Connaught and third son of Queen Victoria, after whom the school was named, was also Governor General from 1911-1916. The vice-regal party landed at the public wharf where it met a reception committee that included Sir William Van Horne and Senator Mackay. The party walked to the head of the wharf and from there, led by the town band, proceeded by carriage to the school on King Street. In their wake followed an "immense" concourse of people, some of whom, as this photograph demonstrates, had gathered in Market Square. Pupils and teachers lined King Street and at the school itself a school choir sang "The Flag of Britain." The mayor's civic address opened with the phrase: "The citizens of the Loyalist town of St Andrews."

GOLDEN JUBILEE PARADE 1887

Royal birthdays, anniversaries, and British military victories were usually occasions for unrestrained expressions of allegiance and loyalty. On the fiftieth anniversary of the reign of Queen Victoria, May 1881, there was hardly a building that did not display flags, banners, and bunting. For want of a flag, one householder was said to have run out strips of coloured carpet, but for householders and business owners disinclined or unable to do their own decorating there were professionals to do it for them. The ceremonies began with the firing of a salute at the head of King Street by the Woodstock Field battery, and the ringing of town and church bells. People from the rural districts poured into town on foot and by team—150 of the latter according to one count. Others came by train and steamer, packing the streets. Calais provided a band as well as dozens of excursionists and it is likely that the event was celebrated in Calais itself. For the Queen's birthday in 1892 the *St Croix Courier* reported that Calais schoolchildren were given a half-day holiday and the main street was decked with bunting. The *Courier* urged border communities on the Canadian side to reciprocate on the coming Fourth. This photograph, taken at the junction of King and Water streets, shows the formation of the parade.

THE RELIEF OF LADYSMITH

TOP RIGHT

Two of the best-known events of the war in South Africa are the sieges of Ladysmith and Mafeking. Relief came to Ladysmith on February 29, 1901, after a four-month siege, when its 220,000 inhabitants were at their last gasp. Most of the casualties were a result of sickness rather than shellfire. When news of the relief reached St Andrews the town band turned out, but clearly not to a throng of townspeople. Reserves of public emotion may have been drained by the death of the revered Queen Victoria in the previous month. At least one St Andrews man served in South Africa: Edwin P. Mallory joined the New Brunswick Dragoons, fought in the war, and when he returned—with a German wife—he was met by the town band and presented with a silver cup.

CORONATION DAY, 1911

BOTTOM RIGHT

The town band, with its inevitable train of children, is celebrating the coronation of George V, June 22, 1911. This photograph, taken at the junction of Water and William streets, reveals the rich, eclectic mixture of storage sheds and barns behind the stores and houses on the front street.

THE RELIEF OF LADYSMITH

CORONATION DAY, 1911

81   Bands and Parades

THE DEFEAT OF RECIPROCITY, 1911

The 1911 federal election was one of the most divisive in the town's history. The issue was reciprocity, or free trade, with the United States, which was promoted by the ruling Liberal party led by Sir Wilfrid Laurier. The local candidates were William F. Todd for the Liberals and Thomas A. Hartt for the Conservatives. Fishermen and businessmen argued that reciprocity would open the vast American market without in any way damaging trade relations with Britain. Conservatives, on the other hand, led nationally by Robert L. Borden, contended that reciprocity threatened Canada's sovereignty and would inevitably weaken ties with Great Britain and the Empire. A vote for Hartt, as the banner reads, was a vote for the Empire. In Loyalist St Andrews, the vote went against the Liberals by a margin of 71 votes out of 353 cast. Who said, read the message on a contemporary postcard, that St Andrews wasn't loyal? The fishing community of Grand Manan, by contrast, voted overwhelmingly for Laurier. The *St Andrews Beacon*, which supported reciprocity, ignored the reception for Borden at the railway station and the parade down water street that followed it.

THE EDWIN ODELL STORE
TOP RIGHT

Water Street had seldom been so elaborately decorated as on the occasion of the Duke of Connaught's visit. Flags and bunting, often hung by professional decorators, covered houses and store fronts. To celebrate the vice-regal visit in 1912, the Odell store displayed a crown and an ermine robe.

DECORATED HOUSE
BOTTOM RIGHT

This house, built c.1880 in the French Second Empire style, still stands on Water Street. The mansard roof and the dormer windows effectively add a full storey to the building. The decorations were for the Duke of Connaught's visit.

THE EDWIN ODELL STORE

DECORATED HOUSE

Bands and Parades

Armistice Day Parade, 1918

News of the signing of the armistice reached St Andrews at 7:30 A.M. (11:30 A.M. Greenwich time) on Monday November 11, 1918. Within minutes, town and church bells began to peal and continued at intervals for most of the day. The mayor proclaimed the following day a public holiday and a day for celebration. The weather was unusually mild so there was no impediment to the decoration of houses, streets, stores, and public buildings. Market Square and the adjacent parts of Water Street were festooned with lights powered by the dynamo from Mr Davis's movie theatre in the Street & Company building. The Tuesday celebrations began with a morning chorus of church bells accompanied by horns and steam

SPECTATORS ON WATER STREET WAITING FOR THE START OF THE PARADE

whistles from vessels in the harbour. At noon, a requisitioned canon fired a twenty-one-gun royal salute from the west point blockhouse. The parade proper began at two o'clock, forming at Market Square and moving west along Water Street, north to Montague and then east to the railway station. From the station, the procession, now a mile long, completed the circuit by returning along Water Street to the square. At the head of the parade, which featured floats of a tank and a submarine chaser, were returned soldiers and survivors of the Fenian raid. That night an effigy of the Kaiser was burned by the light of many bonfires and to the strains of band music.

THE PARADE FORMING AT MARKET SQUARE

THE RED CROSS FLOAT PASSING ORDWAYS HALL ON KING STREET

85   Bands and Parades

From the late nineteenth century until the 1960s St Andrews was never without a band. The bands formed and re-formed, playing in parades and, on Sunday evenings, in the bandstand on the green in front of the courthouse.

THE ST ANDREWS BRASS BAND, 1895

LEFT

THE ST ANDREWS TOWN BAND, 1916

BELOW

"Heart and Hand" Fire Brigade, 1927

Chimney sweeps and firewards were among the first municipal appointees in early New Brunswick communities. The firewards were in charge of particular neighbourhoods or districts, organizing the firefighting when fires occurred. During a fire, they carried a seven-foot-long red staff and a white speaking trumpet emblazoned with the town's name. Although unpaid, they were excused jury duty and statutory labour on the roads. In 1833 St Andrews went a step further by forming a volunteer fire company known as the "Heart and Hand." Each member of the twenty-man brigade undertook to equip himself with axes, ropes, lanterns, and a numbered hat or cap that carried the heart and hand symbol. Marchers in the parade to celebrate the sixtieth anniversary of Confederation are retired members of the company. The bottom photograph shows the hose cart leaving the firehall.

Hose cart leaving the firehall
BELOW

Bands and Parades

"The Farm," 1927

As an advocate of rural life, Grace Helen Mowat seldom missed an opportunity to promote it. The checked fabric, simulating a roof, also promoted Cottage Craft, her cottage industry.

Forest Lodge Float

In 1927 Forest Lodge, a house built early in the nineteenth century by the Chamcook merchant and shipbuilder John Wilson, was a popular tourist home. The vehicle is thought to have been a horse-drawn carriage mounted on a chassis, then motorized.

ST ANDREWS SCOUT TROOP

The St Andrews scout troop marching toward the station to meet Lord Willenden, the Governor General, who had come to town to attend the sixtieth anniversary parade. In the photograph below, Lord Willenden inspects an honour guard. The boy scout movement had been founded in 1908 by Lord Baden-Powell, the defender of Mafeking.

LORD WILLENDEN INSPECTS THE HONOR GUARD.

OFFICERS AND MEN OF THE HMS NORFOLK

HMS *Norfolk*, the flagship of the British West Indies Squadron, spent a week in St Andrews in September 1933 as part of a goodwill voyage that included stops in New York, Boston, Saint John, Halifax, Quebec City, and Montreal. With a crew of seven hundred officers and men, it was the largest warship ever to visit the town. In these two photographs taken on the town wharf and on Water Street, officers and men are on their way to church: Roman Catholics to the Church of St Andrew, Anglicans and others to All Saints Church. At All Saints the lessons were read by the commander of the *Norfolk*, Vice-Admiral Drax.

Historical pageant, 1935

The celebrations to mark the Silver Jubilee, the twenty-fifth anniversary of the reign of George V, were probably the most remarkable in the history of the town. There were two main events, a pageant and a grand parade. The pageant was the inspiration of the Imperial Order of the Daughters of the Empire (IODE) who, in response to an appeal from the Lieutenant Governor that the celebrations be enlightening, represented the highlights of British history. At 9:00 A.M. on the day of the pageant, to the accompaniment of a "joyous peal of bells," a young standard bearer in a scarlet suit followed by a herald and pages emerged from the doors of Prince Arthur School. Then followed this remarkable procession: a flaxen-haired Boadicea carrying a golden bow and arrows; a white-robed Julius Caesar bearing an eagle and followed by Roman legionaries; Saxons and Vikings with winged helmets, battle axes, and metal-plated tunics; a sword-bearing William the Conqueror; crusaders in chain armour and tunics, each bearing a large red cross and led by Richard the Lionheart; Henry VIII and three of his queens; Roundheads in high black hats and large white collars and courtly Cavaliers in feathered hats and capes; George IV and Queen Charlotte; Queen Victoria and Prince Albert, soldiers in khaki, red cross nurses, a dove of peace (it had been the war to end all wars) and, finally, a very young princess Elizabeth bearing a Union Jack. The procession made its way to Market Square where the various groups in the pageant, arranged in a great arc, were presented to a gathering of schoolchildren and adults.

This photograph shows about one half of the arc. The Crusaders are on the left, Boadicea on the right. The building behind Boadicea, on the site now occupied by the post office, is a former mattress factory that at the time was being used as a warehouse.

Floats in the Grand Parade

LANDING OF THE LOYALISTS
ABOVE

MOTORIZED CRUSADERS
BELOW

The grand parade was an afternoon affair that began at the railway station and, via a route that covered parts of Water, Queen, Montague, Parr, and King streets, ended at Market Square. Here, the floats were judged. Much admired were the jubilee float in white and silver, the Cottage Craft float which featured a lamb of wool, the Loyalist Landing float, and the float Britannia built by the staff at the residence of Sir Thomas Tait. At the head of the parade was the Deer Island Band and among the marchers were firemen, aldermen, and the mayor. An adjunct to the grand parade was a children's parade of doll carriages, toy cars, boats, and wagons. Afternoon band concerts in Market Square and games that included a sack race, an egg race, and a backward race rounded off the daytime festivities. At night there was a bonfire at Indian Point and a well-attended dance.

George Higgins (as John Bull) and Eldon Doon

RIGHT

The Silver Jubilee Sack Race

BELOW

Bands and Parades

THE LAST VICTORY PARADE   The V.E. (Victory in Europe) Day parade, Water Street, May 1945.

V.E. DAY SERVICE   Market Square, May 1945. The stone arch is a war memorial initially built to honour the dead of World War One.

Chapter 7

Summer Hotels

THE NEW ALGONQUIN

The first Algonquin Hotel burned to the ground in 1914. Rebuilding began almost immediately and the new six-storey, 220-room Algonquin opened in June 1915. The floors as well as the main walls were made from poured, reinforced concrete, the partition walls from terra cotta tile and cement plaster, and the roof from fireproof Welsh slate. The design—part Tudor, part Normandy farmhouse and part chateau by Barrett, Blackadar, and Webster of Montreal—has sometimes offended purists, but the new Algonquin with its generous public rooms and dining rooms overlooking fine lawns and gardens was, and remains, a magnificent grand hotel.

THE ARGYLL

Confident of the town's potential as a summer retreat, in 1871 a group of leading business and professional men founded the St Andrews Hotel Company. They bought the eastern commons, at Indian Point, and in 1872 they began digging a foundation on the northern edge of the common near the site of the present-day community college. Investors, however, were difficult to find and the Argyll didn't open until May 24, 1881, Queen Victoria's birthday. The St Andrews hotel was probably the first summer hotel on Canada's east coast and St Andrews's first venture in the tourist trade. Heading the list of attractions was the promise of absolute exemption from hay fever, no small consideration in the days before antihistamines. Hay fever was regarded then as an affliction exclusive to the urban middle classes; country people and the poor were considered immune. Like many of the town's early hotels, the Argyll was destroyed by fire. In March 1892, a chimney fire spread to a parlour on the second floor, and although firemen and volunteers managed to save much of the hotel's furniture, there was not enough water available to save the building.

THE OLD ALGONQUIN

PHOTOS AT RIGHT

In 1883, a syndicate of largely Boston investors (the St Andrews Land Company) bought eighty town lots and some four hundred to five hundred acres of land just outside the old town plat. In 1888 the group began the construction of a new summer hotel, the Algonquin, on a height of land above the town that offered views of both shores of the peninsula. The Algonquin, flying both the Union Jack and the Stars and Stripes, opened with a flourish in late June 1899. In attendance were the Governor General of Canada, the Lieutenant Governor of New Brunswick, and the Governor of Maine. The *Boston Home Journal* found the new hotel (designed by Rand and Taylor of Boston) to be "Old English" in ambience and style but thoroughly American in its appointments. In short, there was nothing old world about the bathrooms and plumbing. In 1903, however, with the new hotel in some financial difficulty, ownership passed to the CPR, whose interest in St Andrews had been growing since its acquisition in 1889 of the New Brunswick and Quebec Railway and the North American Railway. The latter

THE OLD ALGONQUIN, OPENED IN 1899.

THE OLD ALGONQUIN FROM ITS EAST SIDE, BEFORE THE BUILDING OF THE NEW WING.

linked Boston, Bangor, and Saint John. In 1900, following the purchase of the Argyll Hotel property, the company bought the Algonquin and the holdings of the St Andrews Land Company. It increased the number of guest rooms from 80 to 125 by adding two wings. The bottom photograph, taken by William R. Notman of Montreal, is of the east side of the hotel before the building of the new wing. In the background are the Algonquin holiday cottages, built after the CPR's takeover of the hotel and rented by the month or the season.

THE INN In 1907/08 the CPR bought the house built for the managers of the New Brunswick and Quebec (later Canada) Railway near the station at Indian Point. The house was large and gabled, and had deeply wainscotted windows. Renamed "The Inn" and refurbished by Kate Reed, decorator of the CPR's hotels and steamships, it was run as an annex to the Algonquin by Mrs. Atherton, wife of the Algonquin's manager. Reed had a particular affection for the modest and homely inn, and declared that of all the CPR hotels it was the one nearest to her heart. At one end of the dining room was a nook (below) arranged and designed by Kate Reed, who had an affection for homilies.

ALGONQUIN FIRE

In April 1914, a live charcoal from a brazier used by roofers to melt pitch lodged beneath a shingle on the roof of the hotel. While the men were at lunch, the charcoal burned its way through the tarpaper to the underlying boards and roof timbers. The workers returned to a roof in flames and because the hotel's water supply had been cut off for the winter, they had no means of controlling the fire. Fanned by a strong westerly wind, which seems to have been an inevitable accompaniment to fires in St Andrews, the flames quickly engulfed the entire four-storey central wooden section of the hotel. Only the walls and floors of the new concrete wings survived the fire; everything flammable was lost.

CONSTRUCTION WORKERS The contractors for the rebuilding of the hotel were Peter Lyall & Sons of Montreal, who built the hexagonal-shaped tower in the old Algonquin. All the contractors worked under the general supervision of D.A. Mapes, engineer of buildings for the CPR.

STAFF OF THE OLD ALGONQUIN To find staff, Fred A. Jones of Saint John, the first manager of the Algonquin, had to range as far afield as Boston, there being no local pool of experienced help to draw upon.

ALGONQUIN POWER-HOUSE A guiding principle of hotel management is that, if at all possible, work should not be seen to be done. The carpenter's shop and the powerhouse and boilers, built in 1907, were at the rear of the hotel. A laundry was added shortly afterward, discreetly connected to the hotel by an underground tunnel.

BOILER ROOM The hotel boilers were coal-fired with hard coals, when available, from Pennsylvania or Great Britain. Brought up the hill by cart, the coal was stored in hoppers beside the boiler house.

KATY'S COVE

Because of the huge tides and constant upwelling of cold water, the Bay of Fundy is too cold for comfortable bathing. To make a warm, saltwater swimming place, the Algonquin dredged a cove behind the hotel and enclosed it by replacing a railway trestle at the mouth of the cove with a dam and a sluice gate, the latter to control the flow of water. Although salt water was no longer taken as a cure for gout, worms, and gonhorraea, bathing in it it was still thought to be therapeutic. Guests who chose not to swim in the cove could take tepid sea water baths in water pumped directly from the cove into their rooms. In this photograph, taken c.1890, the railway trestle built by the St Andrews and Quebec Railroad Company is clearly visible.

WORK CREW BUILDING THE DAM AT KATY'S COVE, 1906

TOP RIGHT

THE ALGONGUIN MINERAL SPRING

BOTTOM RIGHT

The Algonquin was never a spa in the European sense, but any resort worthy of the name had to be able to offer mineral waters. Some mineral waters were found in a convenient spring (Samson Spring) behind the hotel and, to lend them validity, the spring was covered with a classical portico. Water was hauled daily to the hotel dining room and, when requested, brought by bell boys to guests' rooms.

WORK CREW BUILDING THE DAM AT KATY'S COVE, 1906

THE ALGONQUIN MINERAL SPRING

RECREATION According to *Harper's Monthly*, golf fever began to rage in the United States in the 1890s. One of the afflicted was Robert Gardiner, vice-president of the St Andrews Land Company, who had a nine-hole "links" course laid out along the shore below the Algonquin Hotel. So popular was the game that the

course eventually acquired the full complement of eighteen holes. An additional nine holes adjacent to the eighteen were added when the CPR bought the old alms house property (the poorhouse farm). Public confidence in medicine was at a low point, and so outdoor recreation was regarded as the key to health. Golf, which like croquet and tennis allowed women to exercise freely without any loss of decorum, was popular with both sexes. The top photograph was taken at the eighth hole of the original course; the caddies were usually boys or young men from the town. The lower photograph is of the clubhouse, built by Robert S. Gardiner at his own expense in 1893. Although unused for decades, it is still in its original location and is now being restored.

Chapter 8

Summer Houses

QUEEN ANNE COTTAGE

It was the intention of the St Andrews Land Company to divide the eastern commons into sixty house or cottage lots that would be supplied with electricity and water, but only one show or model cottage, in the Queen Anne style, was ever built. In 1890 this cottage was moved to the corner of Elizabeth and Carleton streets where it was renamed Algonquin Cottage and advertised for sale or rent by the Land Company. Since 1900 the house has been privately owned, and, despite extensive additions and alterations, parts of the original structure remain intact. This photograph shows the house, still unaltered, in its Parr-Carleton Street location.

THE OLD TOWN AND THE NEW Several architectural periods are represented in this photograph, taken from the spire of Greenock Church c. 1900. In the immediate foreground is Greenock House, brick-built, stocky, and quintessentially Georgian; across the street is an upright, steep-roofed Victorian house with a pointed gable and vertical or Gothic lines; in the middle background is the Land Company's Queen Anne style cottage; and, on the far left, sits the first Algonquin hotel, built in the picturesque American "shingle" style.

LAZY CROFT Lazy Croft, built in 1893 by George and Julia Inness Jr. of New York, was one of the first summer houses in St Andrews. Long and narrow, with interior walls studded with large rivets and a few bedrooms that could only be reached by a narrow outside balcony, Lazy Croft was said to express George Inness's love of ships. Inness was the son of the renowned American landscape painter George Inness, who spent a few summers in St Andrews. Lazy Croft was destroyed by fire in 1972.

COVENHOVEN Eight years before his retirement in 1899, Sir William Van Horne, builder of the Canadian Pacific Railway, bought one end of Minister's Island, an offshore island connected to the mainland by a bar that is exposed at low tide. By 1893 a large gang of men were building roads and digging wells and foundations for a twenty-eight-room mansion-house and outbuildings. A man of parts, Sir William was his own architect, but in 1898/99 design problems led to the engagement of Edward Maxwell, a young Montreal architect. Covenhoven was completed in 1901.

SIR WILLIAM VAN HORNE

BAR ROAD HALT

For their summer visits the Van Hornes arrived at low tide in Sir William's custom-built railcar, the Saskatchewan. They were met at the Bar Road halt by carriages that conveyed them across the exposed bar to the island.

THE BARN AT COVENHOVEN

BELOW

Van Horne's role at Covenhoven was that of gentleman farmer and horticulturist. He imported a herd of Dutch-belted (black and white) cattle and built a massive barn, three storeys high, with turreted silos, a shingled roof with flared gable ends, and a freight elevator. The barn workers wore long white lab coats and at the end

of each work day they sprinkled fresh sawdust on the floors. To design and manage the gardens at Covenhoven, Van Horne engaged Henry Clarke, an Englishman trained at Kew. Clarke introduced the English cucumber to the region and, by crossing a peach with a plum, invented the nectarine. He also grew exceptionally large pears and, to prevent damage to the ripe fruit, he spread nets beneath the trees.

WINDMILL AT COVENHOVEN BELOW

WILLIAM CORNELIOUS COVENHOVEN VAN HORNE

Sir William Van Horne had only one grandchild, the son of Richard Benedict (Bennie) Van Horne and Edith Molson. Sir William is said to have spoiled him unashamedly and when travelling sent him a postcard daily. A capable amateur painter, Van Horne often represented himself as an elephant. This photograph was taken at Covenhoven when William Cornelius was aged three.

FORT TIPPERARY

TOP RIGHT

The CPR's heavy investment in St Andrews and the presence of Sir William Van Horne were magnets that attracted several other CPR executives. In 1902 Sir Thomas Shaughnessy, Van Horne's successor as president of the CPR, and Lady Shaughnessy, built Fort Tipperary, their summer house in St Andrews. As the name suggests, the house occupied the site of the original fort; the old fort was demolished and the new house built inside the grass-covered ramparts. Edward Maxwell, the Montreal architect, made some drawings for the Shaughnessys, but they were not used. The name of the architect of Fort Tipperary has eluded researchers but he is thought to have been a member of the CPR staff.

LORD SHAUGHNESSY WITH FAMILY AND FRIENDS

BOTTOM RIGHT

FORT TIPPERARY

LORD SHAUGHNESSY WITH FAMILY AND FRIENDS

Summer Houses

TILLIETUDLEM The work at Covenhoven was the first of more than a dozen commissions that Maxwell would be offered in St Andrews. Attracted to the town, he bought, at Van Horne's suggestion, five acres of shoreland across from Minister's Island and built a summer house, Tillietudlem, for himself and his young family. In Canada, Maxwell was the leading exponent of the American shingle style. He had completed his training with the Boston firm of Shepley, Rutan & Coolidge, who had taken over the practice of Henry Hobson Richardson, the originator of the style. To escape what he regarded as the inhibiting regularity and formality of classicism, Richardson experimented with new forms, capping his houses with long roofs and almost medieval arrangements of dormers, chimneys, and gables. He covered all exterior surfaces, including supporting pillars, with rough shingles.

HILLCREST
TOP RIGHT

The summer or "fun" houses, as Maxwell described them, were built just before the World War One when the rich, unburdened by taxes and untroubled by ostentation, built grand summer houses. In St Andrews the summer houses create a decorative horsehoe around the old town plat. In keeping with their function, they often bear romantic and even playful names: Clibrig, Berwick Brae, Les Goelands, Tillietudlem, Pansy Patch. Hillcrest, although plainly named, is an exemplar of the style. Designed by Edward Maxwell and his brother William, its turrets, verandahs, steeply pitched roofs, and shingle covering are reminders that though grand, the house is a summer one. It was built in 1905 for C.R. Hosmer who was then head of the CPR's telegraph department.

ROSEMOUNT
BOTTOM RIGHT

Rosemount, built on a property that adjoins Hillcrest, was a Maxwell commission that called for the design not only of the main building but also of the interior, the furniture, and the garden. Its owner was Englishman Charles Smith, who first came to St Andrews in 1861 with his regiment, en route to Quebec. After retiring in England, Smith returned to Canada, and in 1907 built Rosemount.

HILLCREST

ROSEMOUNT

Summer Houses

TOPSIDE

The builder of Topside, Thomas Wheelock, lived for many years in Shanghai where he owned a fleet of lighters that loaded and unloaded ocean-going vessels at the mouth of the Yangtze River. On their first visits to St Andrews, the Wheelocks stayed at the Argyll Hotel; they built Topside in 1897. Their daughter, Florence Wheelock Ayscough, a writer and Sinologue, built the chapter house and tearoom on Water Street for the I.O.D.E. Lucille Douglas, who painted the murals for the tea room, was a friend of Mrs Ayscough and the illustrator of *Firecracker Land*, one of Florence Ayscough's best-known books.

PANSY PATCH

TOP RIGHT

When advertised for sale in 1927, Pansy Patch was said to be a copy of Jacques Cartier's House in St Malo. The claim seems dubious but the turret and the steep, dominating roof do suggest the style of Norman and Breton farmhouses. But resemblance ends there, for Pansy Patch, designed by Charles Sax in 1912 for Hayter and Kate Reed, was a quintessential "fun" house, though subsequently it has served as a year-round dwelling, a rare book shop, an inn, and a restaurant. The verse in a sampler of Pansy Patch embroidered by Kate Reed opens with the lines: "*We built a little cottage and fenced it round about / with quietude and happiness to keep our troubles out.*" Hayter Reed, a former Commissioner for Indian Affairs, was manager-in-chief of the CPR hotels and Kate Reed, a connoisseur of furniture and fine arts, was their chief decorator.

CORY COTTAGE

BOTTOM RIGHT

Cory Cottage, which is next door to Pansy Patch, was originally a farmhouse, built about 1830. Kate and Hayter Reed bought the property in 1915 and remodelled both the house and the garden. The figure in the photograph is Gordon Reed, the son of Hayter and Kate Reed, and owner of Cory cottage. The garden of Cory Cottage, a combination of formal paths and flower beds and more naturalistic arrangements of planted trees and shrubs, was characteristic of the eastern seaboard resorts.

PANSY PATCH

CORY COTTAGE

Notes

Unless indicated otherwise, all photos appear courtesy of the Charlotte County Archives.

INTRODUCTION

PAGE NO.

i	Lithograph of St. Andrews	73#1
vii	St. Croix or Dochet's Island	184#3
ix	Queen Charlotte	173#1
ix	George III	173#2

Chapter 1: HOUSES AND RESIDENTIAL STREETS

1	Chestnut Hall	84#1
2	Panoramic View	245#188 Neg. 2006
	photograph D. Will McKay	
3	Jeremiah Pote's House	129#38
3	The Loyalist House	
	N.B. Museum/Sandy Smith Collection	
4	The Rigby House	310#6
5	Robert Garnett's House	129#45
5	Dunn-McQuoid House	75#6
6	Pagan-O'Neill House	129#9
7	The Sheriff Andrews/Hibbard House (2)	
7	George Hibbard House	
	Ralph Hibbard Goodchild Collection	
8	Harris Hatch House	218#263
9	Greenock House	230#163
9	The Anchorage	230#126
10	Lower King Street	214#1
11	Upper King Street	189#4
11	Upper King Street	129#22
	photograph D. Will McKay	
12	Sophia Street	69#97
13	Milton Hall	
	Sandy Smith Collection	
13	Marine Hospital	46#11
14	Captain Clark's House	308#
	photograph Isaac Erb, Provincial Archives	

Chapter 2: WATER STREET

15	Water Street	69#439
16	Water Street	69#438
17	Fire at Edwin Odell's Store	92#2
	photograph Robert L. Young	

PAGE NO.			
	18	The N.B. Liquor Store	92#1
		photograph Robert L. Young	
	19	Wren's Drug Store	69#445
	19	Street & Company	158#1
	20	The Kennedy Hotel	230#11
	21	Cottage Craft	221#14
	22	Bolts of Cloth	221#35
	22	Lord Byng at Chesnut Hall	221#37
	23	Niger Reef Teahouse	23#1
	25	The Mallory House and Livery Stable	250#2
	25	The Mallory House and Livery Stable	250#5
	26	The Mallory Bus	250#3
	27	Blacksmith's Shop	200#1
	27	Land Company Office	245#120
	28	Eleanor Roosevelt (1933)	282#81
	29	Eleanor Roosevelt with Sir Thomas Tait	282#79
		photograph John O'Neill	
	30	Woman with Pony and Trap	128#1
	31	Fire Station and the Old Town Hall (1927)	121#1
	32	The Windsor House	68#5
	33	J. Ross, Shoemaker	245#122 Neg 2095
	34	The Old Coffee House	264#4

Chapter 3: THE WATERFRONT

	35	Doone's Fish Wharf and Factory	246#8
	36	The Shoreline	184#8
	37	Rock Picking at O'Neill's Farm (Nov 10,1910)	
		photograph A.A. Shirley	
		George Goodeill collection	
	37	Chamcook Weir	
	38	Seining a Weir	111#2
	38	Loading Herring Into a Carrier	297#27
	39	Sardine Cannery, Chamcook	218#22
	40	Boarding Houses, Chamcook	218#221
	41	Cod Flakes Drying at Doone's Wharf	246#9
	41	Bringing in the Catch	240#3
	42	Greenlaw's Fish Factory	90#32
	43	Conley's Lobster Plant	208#15
	44	A Moveable Biological Station	
	44	A Permanent Marine Biological Station	
	45	Attic in the Old Laboratory	
	45	Library in the Old Laboratory	
	46	Repairing Lobster Traps	
		photos pages 44-46 Biological Station	
		Collection, St Andrews	

PAGE NO.			
	47	Railway Trestle	129#7
	47	Hulks and Rotting Wharves	50#1
		photograph D. Will McKay	
	48	Coal-Carrying Schooners	129#26
	49	Captain of the Grand Manan	264#14
	49	The *Rose Standish*	184#7
	50	Hoist on the Market Wharf (1942)	
		Irma Thompson Collection	
	50	Pendlebury Light	283#53

Chapter 4: MEN IN UNIFORM

	51	Ready for War!	290#40
	52	Three Military Gentlemen	129#10
	53	West Point Blockhouse	69#389
		photograph William R. Notman	
	54	A Mothballed Blockhouse	282#1
	55	One of the Twenty-four-Pounders	282#62
	55	Fort Tipperary, 1890	129#55
	56	St Andrews Rifle Company 1861-65	69#437
	57	Militia at Ease, c. 1860	7#1
	57	Militia on Parade, c. 1860	23#49
	58	Summer Camp	184#14
	58	Summer Camp	184#11
	59	Departure of the Volunteers	264#19
	59	Departure of the Volunteers	264#17
	60	Lone Soldier and Blockhouse	286#158-246
	61	Visiting Day	127#12
	62	Captured German Gun	69#329
	62	Cavalrymen	296#182
		photograph A.A. Shirley	
	63	Private Vincent McQuoid	75#111
	64	A Call to Arms, 1940	69#506
	64	Witnesses to the Call	69#505

Chapter 5: CHURCHES, SCHOOLS, AND PUBLIC BUILDINGS

	65	Chapel of Ease of Saint John the Baptist	
	66	All Saints Church	184#15
	67	Greenock Church	
	68	Loyalist Burying Ground	245#50 Neg 1215
	69	The Church of St Andrew	112#1-11
	69	United Baptist Church	297#10 or 218#95
	70	The Second Church of St Andrew	282#106
	71	Wesleyan United Church	69#3
	72	The St Andrews Grammar School	282#87
		photograph A.A. Shirley	

PAGE NO.			
	72	Classroom in the Old Grammar School	189#32
	73	The First Elementary School	129#48
	74	Intermediate School	151#1
	75	Prince Arthur School	282#114
	75	Prince Arthur School	266#35
	76	Learning the Lessons	213#1
	76	Learning the Lessons	68#5
	77	Charlotte County Gaol	105#1
	77	Charlotte County Gaol (interior view)	
	78	Charlotte County Courthouse	282#98
	78	Ordways Hall (1927)	282#73

Chapter 6: BANDS AND PARADES

	79	The Arrival of the Duke of Connaught, 1912	8#1
	80	Golden Jubilee Parade, 1887	184#21
	81	The Relief of Ladysmith	245#1
	81	Coronation Day, 1911	245#28
	82	The Defeat of Reciprocity, 1911	245#146
	83	The Edwin Odell Store	290#36
		photograph D. Will McKay	
	83	Decorated House	122#5

The Armistice Day Parade:

	84	Spectators on Water Street	218#205
	85	Parade Forming at Market Square	218#106
	85	The Red Cross Float	218#109
	86	The St Andrews Brass Band, 1895	56#1
	86	The St Andrews Town Band, 1916	107#3
	87	Heart and Hand Fire Brigade, 1927	121#3
	87	The Hose Cart Leaving the Firehall	121#2
	88	"The Farm," 1927	228#15
	88	Forest Lodge Float	121#6
	89	St Andrews Scout Troop	228#21
	89	Lord Willenden Inspects an Honour Guard	228#22
	90	Officers and Men of the HMS *Norfolk*	218#51
	90	Officers and Men	218#52
	91	Historical Pageant	245#35
		photograph A.A. Shirley	

Floats in the Grand Parade:

	92	Landing of the Loyalists	245#37
	92	Motorized Crusaders	282#145
	93	George Higgins as John Bull	224#23 or 282#16?
	93	The Silver Jubilee Sack Race	245#43 Neg 628
	94	The Last Victory Parade (1945)	123#2
	94	VE Day Service	123#3 Neg 1583

119   Notes

PAGE NO.		
Chapter 7: SUMMER HOTELS		
95	The New Algonquin	69#390
	photograph Robert L. Young	
96	The Argyll	283#54
97	The Old Algonquin	69#246
	photograph William B. Notman	
97	The Old Algonquin	110#1
	photograph William B. Notman	
98	The Inn	69#430
98	The Dining Room Nook	150#1
99	Algonquin Fire	153#3 or 230#23
99	Algonquin Fire (aftermath)	230#26
100	Construction Workers	161#1
	photograph A.A. Shirley	
100	Staff of the Old Algonquin	52#1
	photograph D. Will McKay	
101	Algonquin Powerhouse	69#393
101	Boiler Room	296#63
102	Katy's Cove	69#388
103	Work Crew, 1906	296#8
103	The Algonquin's Mineral Spring	69#344
104	Recreation: the eighth hole	69#315
104	Recreation: the clubhouse	110#10
Chapter 8: SUMMER HOUSES		
105	Queen Anne Cottage	230#30
106	The Old Town and the New, c.1900	33#34
106	Lazy Croft	110#3
107	Covenhoven	110#5
107	Sir William Van Horne	230#66
	CPR Archives Collection	
108	Bar Road Halt	69#322
108	Barn at Covenhoven	
109	Windmill at Covenhoven	210#2
110	William Cornelius Covenhoven Van Horne	230#68
	photograph William R. Notman	
111	Fort Tipperary	69#374
111	Lord Shaughnessy with family and friends	128#2
112	Tillietudlem	242#7
113	Hillcrest	69#364
113	Rosemount	282#187
114	Topside	69#260
	photograph D. Will McKay	
115	Pansy Patch	69#370
115	Cory Cottage	69#248

120   Historic St Andrews